To Sam and Marion

For their passion

for Israel

Ruth Gruber

7/25/90

BOOKS BY RUTH GRUBER

Haven: The Unknown Story of 1,000 World War II Refugees 1983
Raquela: A Woman of Israel 1978
They Came to Stay 1976
Felisa Rincon de Gautier: The Mayor of San Juan 1972
Israel on the Seventh Day 1968
Science and the New Nations 1961
Puerto Rico: Island of Promise 1960
Israel Today: Land of Many Nations 1958
Israel Without Tears 1950
Destination Palestine: The Story of the Haganah Ship Exodus 1947, 1948
I Went to the Soviet Arctic 1939
Virginia Woolf: A Study 1934

RESCUE

THE EXODUS OF THE ETHIOPIAN JEWS

R E S C U E

THE EXODUS
OF THE
ETHIOPIAN JEWS

by RUTH GRUBER

Atheneum   New York   1987

Atheneum
Macmillan Publishing Company
866 Third Avenue, New York, N.Y. 10022
Collier Macmillan Canada, Inc.

Library of Congress Cataloging-in-Publication Data

Gruber, Ruth, 1911–
    Rescue : the exodus of the Ethiopian Jews.

    1. Falasha Rescue, 1984–1945.   2. Falashas—History.
3. Ethiopia—Emigration and immigration.   4. Israel—
Emigration and immigration.   5. Falashas—Israel.
6. Immigrants—Israel.   7. Israel—Ethnic relations.
I. Title.
DS135.E75G78   963'.004924   87-19262
ISBN 0-689-11771-X

Macmillan books are available at special discounts for bulk purchases for sales promotions, premiums, fund-raising, or educational use. For details, contact:
    Special Sales Director
    Macmillan Publishing Company
    866 Third Avenue
    New York, N.Y. 10022

10 9 8 7 6 5 4 3 2 1

Printed in the United States of America

*To my children Celia and David Michaels
and Barbara and Milton Forman
and to the Ethiopian children who
have already arrived in Israel, and
those still waiting to be rescued.*

Contents

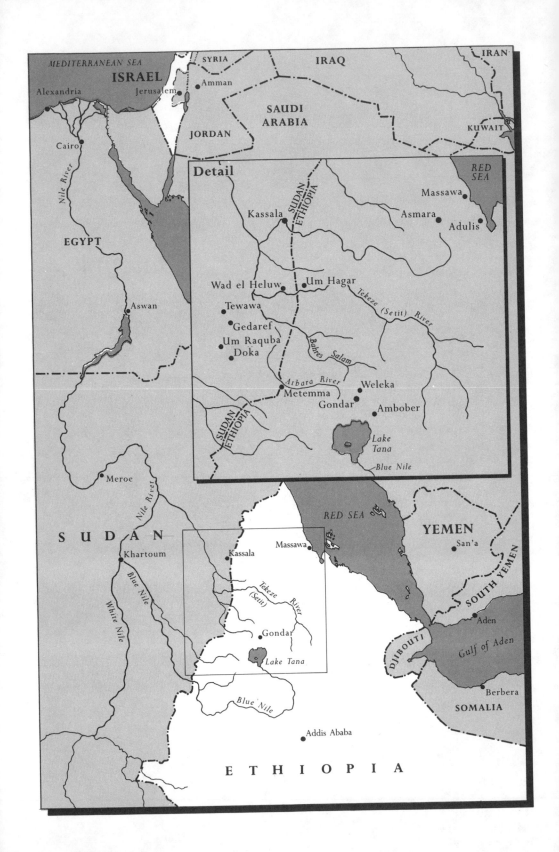

Foreword

O<small>N NEW YEAR'S</small> Day, 1985, I stood on an empty tarmac in Israel and watched a plane land, shrouded in secrecy.

Two hundred fifty black Jews of Ethiopia, wrapped in huge white and desert-colored shawls, stepped out of the aircraft looking as if they had stepped out of Genesis and Exodus.

Operation Moses was underway.

Famine raged in Africa. The Western world, shocked by the photographs of starving children, was shipping billions of dollars in food and medical supplies to feed the dying. But Israel alone, of the nations of the world, was actually rescuing thousands of refugees. For the first time in history, white people were transporting black men and women and children out of Africa not to be sold but to be saved.

I first learned about the Ethiopian Jews, then known as Falashas, in 1948, when I traveled to Israel on a small freighter (planes would no longer fly there) to cover Israel's War of Independence for the *New York Herald Tribune*. On board the ship was Professor Jacques Faitlovitch, a Polish-born French scholar, who was devoting his life to saving the Falashas from extinction.

Each day as we paced the deck, approaching the newborn country fighting against five Arab armies, Professor Faitlovitch described the beauty and nobility of the Falashas, and railed against the world for abandoning the beleaguered heirs of an ancient Jewish kingdom in Africa.

The black Jews of Ethiopia remained part of my consciousness when in 1949 I flew to the Horn of Africa to cover the exodus of the dark-skinned Jews of Yemen for both the *Herald Tribune* and *Look* magazine. For the next four decades, my life was interwoven with refugees as I continued, through thirty-six trips to Israel, the Middle East, and Africa, to write of the tides of immigration that brought a million and a half refugees into Israel.

Covering Operation Moses seemed a natural sequence in my own life and work.

For many years I had enjoyed a warm relationship with Israeli leaders: David Ben-Gurion, Golda Meir, Menachem Begin, Shimon Peres, and Yitzhak Shamir, whose stories I had covered since the end of World War II. Nevertheless it took weeks of knocking on doors until the Mossad, Israel's intelligence agency, granted me permission to meet one of the secret planes, the only American correspondent allowed to watch this last historic exodus.

I then spent months among the Ethiopians in Israel traveling from the Galilee to Beersheba, probing, talking, visiting absorption centers, day-care centers, schools, hospitals, dancing at young people's weddings, sipping tea in their homes, sensing always—so palpable you could touch it—the fear for the safety of their families in Ethiopia and the anguish of their separation.

Then, to trace their stories back to their roots, I made two trips to Ethiopia. I searched for their families in little Jewish villages high in the mountains of Gondar Province. I sat with them, in their straw and mud huts, as they wept with joy looking at the photos I had brought of their children now safe in Israel, and then brought pictures of the families back to Israel with letters and touching gifts.

For the safety of those families in Ethiopia, I have changed the names of nearly all the Ethiopians in the book. But the story of their lives is true.

In cities across the United States, researching the role of the United States in the clandestine rescue, I interviewed current and former American officials, some of whom agreed to talk only on condition that I keep their names anonymous. I have kept that promise.

To the scores of others who have helped in the writing of this book, I give my thanks. Among them are Emma and Graenum Berger, Ora Donio, Howard Eugene Douglas, Jr., Micha Feldman, Elisheva Flamm, Barbara Pfeffer, Yehuda Dominitz, Nina Finkelstein, Milton Forman, Gerold Frank, Moshe Gilboa, Arlene Greco, Rachamin Elazar, Murray Greenfield, Michael Patrick Hearn, Gail Heimberg, Julian Krainin, Richard Krieger, Alaine Krim, Jesse Leiman, Dan Levin, Sarah Levin, Ellen and Harry Lewin, Peggy Mann, Ralph and Marjorie Martin, Abie Nathan, Dr. Chaim Peri, Barbara Ribakove, Barbara Seaman, Irving Schild, Tudor Parfitt, Michael Schneider, Nathan Shapiro, H. Edward Weberman, Helene B. Weintraub, Barry Weise, and especially Russell Galen, my agent, and my editor, Susan Ginsburg, whose enthusiasm spurred this book to completion.

RUTH GRUBER

BOOK ONE
The Escape

Chapter One

ALITASH SAT beside her mother, Adalech, on the earth outside their home, her arms encircling her bare legs, waiting for a tourist to buy her mother's pottery.

Not many tourists came these days to Weleka, the little Jewish village a few miles up the mountains from the ancient city of Gondar. Tourists had been frightened away by the news of rebels fighting government troups in Tigray and Eritrea. Weleka, with some 250 Jews, was in the war zone.

Alitash waited patiently, wrapped in her white shamma—the handwoven cloak that men and women of Ethiopia draped around their bodies like Greek togas or over their heads like prayer shawls. Patience was something she had learned early,

3

for time had little meaning in this village, tucked away in the northwest corner of Ethiopia.

At fifteen, Alitash was a happy, outgoing young woman with a strong open face, a generously wide mouth with dazzling teeth, shining black eyes, and honey-brown skin that glistened as if she had just oiled it. She talked quietly with her mother, who sat serene, like a sculpted, slender matriarch, enclosed in her shamma.

She had a special relationship with her mother. "Always," her mother had told her, "you will be my daughter and my sister, and we will never be apart."

Everything Alitash knew of living she had learned from her thirty-year-old mother, a small, slender woman with a soft voice and short-cropped black hair that sat like a cap on her delicate face. For Adalech, unschooled and illiterate, had passed on to her oldest child the strong family values she had learned from her mother—love and respect for her elders, nurturing little children, living with dignity and honesty and faith.

They sat waiting in the African sun, her mother's soft round eyes beginning to close, when Alitash called out, "Wake up, Mama. A *farangi* [foreigner] is coming up the road. She looks like an American."

Word of the arrival of a tourist spread through the village faster than the beating of a drum. Barefooted and wrapped in their gossamer shammas, the women rushed out of their doors, raced across the earth and stones, and within minutes arranged small clay figurines on a mud ledge at the entrance of the village.

"Hurry," Adalech said. "Bring out more pottery."

Alitash bolted inside their house. It was a simple rectangle that looked like a child's drawing; its walls of mud and dung and straw were interlaced with slats of eucalyptus wood. It had a tin door, a small window, and the much-desired corrugated-tin roof. It was about twenty feet long, with a dirt floor and a narrow ledge of packed mud and straw running around the inner wall. The ledge was for sitting, eating, and

4

sleeping. Two iron cots stood single file high above one part of the ledge. Her parents shared one of the cots; the other was for Alitash. Her ten-year-old sister and her two little brothers slept on the dirt floor. There were no lights, and water from the nearby river stood in a huge jug her mother had crafted.

Racing swiftly to a corner of the house near the water jug, Alitash gathered a handful of little statues, put them in a basket tray, and ran outside, where the women were already hawking their wares. She helped her mother set up the figurines—little black Lions of Judah with Stars of David on their heads, amusing statuettes of pregnant women with their arms around their stomachs, and taller figures of Jewish priests holding prayer books in their hands.

She stood up, hoping to catch the eye of the tourist, impeccably dressed in a safari skirt and jacket with a sun helmet shielding her blond hair and fair skin. A camera hung around her neck like a talisman. She was accompanied by a young man whom Alitash recognized as a government guide from the NTO, the National Tour Operation. In Marxist Ethiopia, no tourist was permitted to travel alone to the Jewish villages.

From where she stood, Alitash could see the woman clicking her camera, smiling as if she were enchanted by the picturesque village with its helter-skelter mud houses, mud paths, and clusters of "tukuls"—African straw huts that looked like oversized birds' nests. The tukuls were protected from the hot sun and the tropical rains by thatched roofs overlapping them like coolie hats.

The woman peeked inside the tukuls. There were no windows, only a low door to let in light. There were no tables or chairs, only the mud bench lining the rounded walls. Smoke from the cooking fires escaped through holes in the thatched roofs and curled up, gray and feathery, into the African sky.

"I think she's coming to us," Alitash alerted her mother. The woman stopped in front of Alitash and Adalech, and removed her sunglasses.

"Ah," she said to her guide, "this is what I'm looking for."

She bent to pick up a small two-inch black clay bed with a tiny naked woman and a naked bearded man embracing, their arms wrapped around each other's bodies. The figures were the Queen of Sheba and King Solomon. Atop the headboard, symbolically hovering over the king and queen, was the Star of David.

Alitash looked gratefully at the tourist and then flashed a radiant smile at her mother.

Of all her mother's pottery, the Queen of Sheba in bed with Solomon was her favorite. For untold generations, Ethiopian children had been told the story that they were the descendants of a night of love between the beautiful black Queen of Sheba and the wise King of Israel. Even the old Christian emperor, Haile Selassie, calling himself the "Lion of Judah," had claimed Solomon and Sheba as his ancestors. The story was Ethiopia's national legend.

Her mother negotiated the price with the tourist. Two birr. (One birr equals fifty cents.) The woman paid the two birr, then, with the NTO guide beside her, returned to the dirt road, took her last photo, and waved good-bye to Alitash and her mother.

THE VILLAGE settled back to wait for another tourist, when Alitash saw Daniel coming up the road, striding regally, like a young king. His head seemed molded on a long slender throat, his lips were finely carved below a thin black mustache, and his dark thoughtful eyes were set wide and deep below thick eyebrows.

"Alitash," he said, "I have to speak with you."

She heard the anxiety in his voice. She asked her mother if she might go with him.

Adalech nodded as the two young people walked barefoot toward the hills that surrounded the village. It was early June, monsoon time, and the beginning of the rainy season. Rain had fallen during the night and then stopped. The tropical morning light played softly on the straw tukuls and the mud houses and, on the hill above them, the synagogue crowned with the Star of David.

The smell of Ethiopia was in the air as they walked, the warm, scented smell of wood burning, dung burning, straw burning. And now, beyond the village, the smell dissolved and the air felt clean and washed, for Weleka lay on a table-top, sixty-seven hundred feet above sea level.

Other days, Alitash loved this walk with Daniel, happy just to be near him. Today she sensed only fear.

He spoke in whispers. "Alitash, I just came back from Gondar. I found out they . . ." he hesitated.

"Yes? Who?"

"The soldiers. They know I tried to help some students get out of the country—the ones who wanted to get to Israel. Now someone warned me, they're planning to arrest me. I've got to get out of the country."

"No. You mustn't—" She stopped.

"Alitash, I don't want to be one of those May Day corpses."

She shuddered. Three years earlier, on May Day in 1977, soldiers and security police had burst into homes across Addis Ababa, the capital city, and pulled high school and university students out of their beds. No reasons were given. Young men and women—Christians, Moslems, and Jews—were arrested and shot on the street or inside prison walls.

It was no accident that the military dictatorship had selected students for their May Day victims. Students could become leaders who might one day lead the people to overthrow the Dergue—the Marxist military council—just as the Dergue had overthrown Emperor Haile Selassie in 1974.

Alitash and Daniel had heard from friends who had escaped the massacre that two thousand had been murdered.

They heard too how high school girls had been dragged into Addis' slums and alleyways filled with human and animal excrement. Soldiers raped the girls and then shot them.

Some of the bodies were left in front of the parents' homes. Other parents had to pay thirty birr for each bullet that was shot into their children before they could retrieve the body of their son or daughter.

"You must leave at once," Alitash whispered.

Daniel took her hand. "I've rounded up fourteen of my high school friends. Will you come with us?"

She turned to look at him. How often, as a little girl listening to her father's stories, had she pictured herself climbing the Holy Mountain in Jerusalem, the place they called Mount Zion, where King Solomon had built his Holy Temple. Could she go now? Could she leave her parents whom she loved? Her little sister? Her two younger brothers? Her best friends?

"Alitash," Daniel pressed, "I want you to come with me."

"How soon must you know?"

"Tonight."

THERE WAS reason for the urgency.

A handful of the twenty-eight thousand Jews of Ethiopia had begun to trickle out secretly, trying to reach Israel, risking their lives. Ethiopia's leader, Lieutenant Colonel Mengistu Haile Mariam, barred emigration, reasoning that if you let the twenty-eight thousand Jews leave, tens of thousands of Christians and Moslems and pagans would clamor to get out.

Politically, Ethiopia was a museum of paradoxes. The oldest empire in Africa had become in the mid-1970s a Marxist-Leninist state. Yet it was still a tribal land, a patch-quilt of some seventy ancient tribes who knew little or nothing about one another and who spoke some two hundred languages and dialects.

It was a nation of 40 million people, 50 percent Christian, 35 percent Moslem, and the rest, besides the twenty-eight thousand Jews, followers of traditional African religions.

The ruling tribe, barely 25 percent of the populace, were

the Christians who spoke Amharic. Haile Selassie, a member of this ruling tribe, had dreamt of blending the seventy tribes into one nation, and westernizing the country.

He had failed.

Now Mengistu, the thirty-five-year-old officer who had been trained in America and won his position by a shootout of his six rivals around a meeting table, dreamt too of blending the tribes into one nation, with socialism the national religion. For this, he needed a closed society. If he opened the gates for twenty-eight thousand Jews, the country could hemorrhage.

But the hemorrhaging had already started. Since 1974, thousands of Ethiopians had begun the flight from war and revolution and terror. In two horror-filled years, from 1977 to 1979, ten thousand were murdered in the name of the revolution.

Of all the countries in the Horn of Africa, Ethiopia was the poorest. There was little birth control, but highly effective death control. Every few years, drought and terrible famine killed tens of thousands of people and their cattle. Thousands more died in the wars with Eritrea and Somalia.

Deaths by starvation, by war, and by execution were the dramatic killers. Less dramatic but more decimating were the diseases of poverty, famine, and filth. There was no census of death, but at least three-quarters of the dying were children under five. Helplessly, parents, often dying themselves, watched their children's bodies wither, their eyes turn opaque with blindness. Any child, malnourished during its first six years of life, was almost inevitably brain-damaged.

So the people had begun running out of Ethiopia, trying to escape.

The Christians and Moslems who lived close to the border with Sudan were fortunate. In the dark of night, they could find areas with no patrols, and slip across to safe haven.

The Jews were less fortunate. Most of them had settled in

9

mountain villages far from Sudan. To escape, they had to travel hundreds of miles to reach the border. On the way, soldiers and police often tracked them down. Many were imprisoned. Some were killed.

The Marxist regime could pretend to be unaware of the flight of most of the refugees. But the exodus of the Jews was an embarrassment to the government. Of the thousands who had fled to the camps in Sudan, the Jews were the only ones who had a place to go—Israel—anathema to the Communist regime.

In the politics of escape, the Jews had to be singled out, deterred, made special scapegoats.

Daniel had to flee.

BACK IN THE village, Alitash was in turmoil. Whom could she talk to? Who could help her make the most important decision of her life?

She sought out her best friend, Malka. She found her inside her house, grinding coffee. Malka, fifteen, was the beauty of Weleka, tall, with delicately carved features in an oval face, self-possessed. Growing up in the little village of Weleka, she had shown rare qualities for an Ethiopian girl. Courageous, forthright, artistic, with a flare for decoration, she had covered the mud walls of the house with Tourism Commission posters of Ethiopia's breathtaking landscapes and smiling bare-breasted women. Even in this rainy season, the posters proclaimed in English: ETHIOPIA—THIRTEEN MONTHS OF SUNSHINE.

Alitash spoke rapidly: "Malka, listen. Daniel is in danger. He's leaving for Israel with fourteen friends. He wants me to go with him."

"What did you tell him?" Malka demanded.

"I didn't know what to tell him. I have to let him know tonight."

"There's no question. You must go."

"But to leave everyone—my friends—you . . . !"

Malka put her arms around Alitash. "Daniel isn't the only one in danger. You're in danger; we're all in danger."

"I know." Alitash's voice was hoarse with fear.

"You know how they hate educated people," Malka said. "They could round up every high school student and murder us all."

"But what about school? I want to finish—"

"You can finish school in Israel. I might even . . ." Malka paused, then stared at the Ethiopian posters on the wall.

"You might what?" Alitash asked.

"I might go too."

"Would you?"

"Here I am trying to convince you to go," Malka said, "and I'm convincing myself."

Alitash's knees were shaking. "It would be so good—"

Malka's voice was firm. "I'm going."

"And what about our friends? Yael. Zehava. Judith. We five have been together since we were little children."

"I'll ask them," Malka said. "Maybe all of us will go."

At home, Alitash said nothing to her mother. She decided to wait until her father returned at dusk. Then she could confront them together. Her forty-year-old father, Solomon, had gone to the Gondar market to buy grain.

Alitash's mind churned as she helped her mother prepare the food for supper. Would her parents give her permission to leave? And even if all her friends agreed to go, would *their* parents give permission? Five girls traveling alone with fifteen young men, unchaperoned? It was unheard of in the Jewish villages. Parents guarded the purity of their daughters so carefully that any girl who was not a virgin on her wedding night was instantly divorced, shunned, and sometimes cast out of the village.

Inside the house, her mother bent over a heavy pot. She was cooking the heavily spiced stew of grains and vegetables and red-hot pepper called *wot*. On special days she added meat to the spicy stew. But this was an ordinary day.

"Alitash," her mother said. "Do go outside and make injera."

Injera was the native bread of Ethiopia, a rubbery pancake that was the basis of all their meals.

Work helped Alitash curb the turmoil in her brain. She built an open fire on a stone hearth, placed a large clay cooking platter over the fire, and greased the platter. When the fire was so hot she could no longer touch the platter, she poured onto it a mixture of water and fermented *teff*, the native, tiny-seeded grass that grows nearly three feet high.

She forced herself to concentrate as she covered the platter with a high lid made of clay and straw. Within seconds, the mixture began to bubble, the bubbles broke, and in less than three minutes, the first pancake was finished. She cooked a dozen or more and brought them into the house to cool off.

At dusk, Solomon returned, tired from the long walk home from Gondar.

"Everything smells so good," he said. "I'm ready to eat and rest."

He looked affectionately at his family, then settled himself on the ledge closest to the door, where Adalech joined him. Parents ate first and alone in the Jewish villages. It was part of the respect for one's elders instilled into every Jewish child.

From one of her mother's earthenware jugs, Alitash poured water over her parents' hands. Then they lifted the pancakes onto their communal plate and waited as she spooned out the boiling hot stew.

There were no forks or knives. They dipped small pieces of injera into the hot and spicy sauce, and when they finished, Alitash served her younger sister and her little brothers.

"You're not eating anything," Adalech noticed.

"I'm not hungry today," she said. She cleaned the plate and hung the pots on nails on the mud wall.

Finally, it was time to speak.

"Daniel is going to Jerusalem with fourteen boys. He must go immediately. Soldiers are looking for him."

She paused, watching their faces fill with concern for Daniel. Then she blurted out, "I want to go with them."

Her mother looked stricken. "Alitash, how can we let you go? Who will protect you?"

"Daniel will, Mother. You know him well. You can trust him."

Solomon spoke. "I can understand that Daniel must go. His life is in danger. But why must you go?"

"Father, all these years you taught me about Jerusalem. You told me how every Jew dreams of climbing the Holy Mountain in the Holy City. I will be the first in our family to climb the mountain. Then, if God wills, all of you can come too."

Her father sighed painfully. "But how many have ever reached Israel?"

Her mother put her face in her hands. "We hear such terrible stories about what happens to people trying to escape. How will I know you're safe?"

"I'll write to you as soon as I reach the Holy Land."

"Letters! Letters can take months—if they even arrive."

Adalech turned on her husband. "It's your fault that this is happening. You put all these ideas into her head. You're the one who said she's so smart, she should finish sixth grade here and even go to high school."

"And now she's in the ninth grade," Solomon said, "and I'm proud of her going to high school."

Alitash listened in silence. Five evenings a week, she walked three miles to the high school in Gondar city, after helping Adalech cook and clean and sew and weave baskets and fashion little Queens of Sheba in bed with King Solomon. It was a dark road to Gondar, often preempted by wild animals and gangs of bandits. But Alitash walked unafraid, excited that she was learning English—all high school classes in Ethiopia were held in English.

"High school!" Adalech spat out the words. "Most girls her age are already married."

"Yes," her father said. "Betrothed at nine, married at twelve, pregnant at thirteen, mothers at fourteen, and often dead at thirty-five. I see them when I pass the hospital in Gondar, sick, worn-out, dying."

Solomon stood up and put his hand on Alitash's shoulder. "You're right—this was my dream, and my father's dream before me, and my grandfather's—to reach Jerusalem. They didn't know, nor did I, that the first one in our family to go would be a daughter. I give you our blessings."

Adalech leaped from the ledge, raising her voice. Alitash had never heard her so angry and bitter. "Why do you give her permission? My first-born. What are you sending her to? To be arrested by soldiers? To be raped by bandits? To be eaten by strange animals? I can't bear to think of what can happen to her if she goes."

"And I'm thinking of what can happen to her if she stays. They can start shooting high school students again." He looked at his wife. "Adalech, we must let her go."

"This is a terrible thing we have to decide on."

Adalech lowered herself to the floor, surrendering to helpless, soul-wrenching sobs. Alitash bent beside her, wiping the tears from her face. "Mother, don't. Please don't cry."

Adalech pushed her away. "Then go. But I shall never sleep again without worrying—is Alitash still alive?"

Alitash's throat went dry. "I will be safe, Mother. I will write to you. Trust me."

Blindly, she ran from the house.

In Malka's house, she said simply, "I have permission to go."

"I too," Malka reported. "There was no trouble. My father said, 'Go, with my blessings.' "

"And the others?"

"It wasn't so easy, but finally they won their parents over."

"You mean—everyone—everyone is coming?"

"Yes. All of us. We're all going to make *aliyah*."

Aliyah—"the going up." The going up from slavery to freedom. The going up from Ethiopia to Israel.

The dream of *aliyah* was sweeping the Jewish villages. The few hundred young people who were already in Israel had been writing letters urging their families and friends to come.

Alitash had seen one of the letters describing Israel. "It's a magic land where people are free. Come by whatever means you can, legally if you can get a passport. Otherwise come illegally. But come."

DANIEL WAS home preparing for the journey when Alitash entered.

"I'm going with you," she said.

He flung his arms around her.

"And my best friends are coming too," she said.

"What?" He stepped back. "How many?"

"Four plus me."

"Five girls." Daniel was dismayed. "Do you have any idea how hard this journey will be? I love you, Alitash. It's you I want. Five girls." He shook his head. "It's too dangerous. Crossing mountains, deserts, robbers, soldiers—they can kill us all."

"I won't go without them."

Daniel paced the earth floor. "If we take the five of you," he said thoughtfully, "plus the fourteen boys coming with me, we will be twenty. That's a bigger group than I planned." He shook his head. "Can five girls make it?"

"Daniel, we're not breakable," she tossed her black hair. "We're not clay like my mother's little figures."

She reached for him. "You can't leave without me. You know that. There's trouble with my mother. She's turned against me. But I'm going. And my friends are going. It's our *aliyah* too."

He took her hand in his. "You are strong, Alitash. The

thought of starting a new life without you would make me crazy."

Alitash brushed his lips with her fingertips. "I love you, Daniel."

They stood silently, clutching each other. Alitash lay her head against his chest. "When do we go?" she asked.

"Sunday."

She looked up. "In three days! Can you get ready so fast?"

"We have to. I could be arrested any day."

"We'll be ready," she said. "What do I take?"

"As little as possible. Not even a pencil. Just what you have on your back. And your wristwatch."

Alitash looked down at her wrist. The watch was her prize possession. The watch that told her when to be in school.

"I'm going to Gondar City tomorrow," Daniel said, "I have to shop for food and supplies and medicine. Will you come along and help me?"

"I'll come."

He drew a purse from the pocket of his jeans. "Look. Eighty birr."

"How did you get it all?"

Daniel said, "Some came from the group. The rest is money I earned working for ORT."

ORT—the worldwide Jewish Organization for Rehabilitation Through Training—had begun its operations in Ethiopia in 1976, two years after the revolution. Sorely in need of help, the Marxist government had accepted ORT's offer to set up a rural development program. The one condition the government demanded was that ORT help the whole population, not only the Jews. ORT readily agreed.

Daniel had become one of ORT's apprentice carpenters in Weleka. And both Alitash and her mother had studied in the ORT pottery workshop, learning how to press the foot pedal, turn the potter's wheel, and fashion their little Queens of Sheba and King Solomons.

Now Daniel anchored the purse with the ORT money deep

into his pocket. Then, with one hand he embraced Alitash while with the other he fingered her hair, stroked her copper-gold cheeks, and gently outlined her lips.

In his arms, she heard her mother's voice. *Why did you give her permission? She is my first-born.*

They were still embracing when the roar of a jeep speeding on the dirt road burst like a gunshot into the quiet village.

Through the doorway, they watched Major Malaku, the governor of Gondar Province, a short, handsome black warlord, racing his jeep around the bend into the village.

Malaku's arrival at any hour of the day or night sent the Jewish villages into spasms of fear. He was one of the founders of the revolution, part of the military junta that had overthrown the emperor in 1974. As a reward, he was given the governorship of the province of Gondar.

Honking the horn of his jeep as though he were beating it, he shouted, "Come out. All of you."

The people stepped fearfully out of their houses, drawing their shammas over their faces so that only their eyes showed.

"You parents"—Malaku, dressed in a black leather jacket and black leather boots, stood up in his jeep, shouting—"listen well. Some of your sons and daughters are stealing out of the villages and trying to reach the Zionist imperialist land of Israel. I warn you. If I find any of your children missing, I will hold you responsible. You are the ones who will go to prison, unless your sons and daughters come back."

So now their parents were as much in danger as they were. Malaku had already captured some of the young people trying to flee. He had thrown them into prison, and tortured some of them.

His favorite torture was the bastinado. Prisoners were hung upside down and then beaten with clubs on the soles of their feet. Hot oil was poured on their wounds to prevent healing. Women prisoners were given special torture with hot oil poured into their vaginas.

"Remember"—Malaku cracked his black riding stick into

the air—"if I hear that any of your sons or daughters have left for that imperialist Zionist country, I will personally have you arrested and tortured."

With a roar of his engine, he raced his jeep down the road.

"You still want to go?" Daniel asked.

She nodded silently, unable to speak.

Chapter Two

EARLY THE NEXT morning, Alitash and Daniel set out on their shopping expedition. Alitash's father had given her a purse with forty birr. "Buy whatever you need," he had said. "And be sure to buy sandals. You can't trek to Sudan barefoot."

Gondar, two miles down the winding dirt road from Weleka, was the limit of their world. Neither of them had ever been beyond this mountain city.

It was here that Alitash had first learned of the wonders of running water and bathrooms and electricity and newspapers and television. For Weleka had none of these.

Some eighty thousand people lived in the city, most of them in crowded shantytowns of mud huts set in the folds of undulating green hills. The jumble of tin roofs sparkled silver in the morning sun.

Government officials and the few who had money lived in pastel-colored villas with graceful balconies and shuttered windows. The villas, a historic reminder, had been built by the Italians in the five years from 1936 to 1941 when Mussolini had occupied the country.

Approaching Gondar as the road twisted precariously around the steep hills, Alitash looked up at the wall of the old imperial city. In her history class, she had learned how in 1636 the Emperor Fasiladas had moved the capital from the ancient stronghold of Aksum near the Red Sea and made Gondar, this city in the mountains, the capital of the country.

He had brought in architects from Portugal who designed his massive medieval castles, unique in black Africa, with henna-brown crenellated stone towers and battlemented walls. But he needed no imported labor to build the castles, for he used his own Jewish artisans and craftsmen, his "Falashas."

More than two hundred years ago, in 1770, the artistry and skill of the Falashas had won them the admiration of the Scotch explorer James Bruce. Visiting the reigning emperor and his harem, Bruce described the castle whose "ceiling in gayety and taste was the work of the Falasha, and consisted of painted cane, split and disposed in Mosaic figures, which produces a gayer effect than it is possible to conceive."

Dozens of people were on the street as Alitash and Daniel made their way along the winding main thoroughfare toward the marketplace. Horse-drawn primitive carts, called "Gondar taxis," with half-naked drivers whipping their horses, churned up the dust.

Donkeys blocked their path, cows strolled leisurely, soldiers from the nearby tent barracks marched in formation, and beggars and shoeshine boys called out to them as they walked on the unpaved street of dirt and loose gravel past the post office and the bank and the government buildings in one of which, they were sure, Major Malaku ruled, until finally they reached the great open-air market which seemed to stretch to the horizon.

Alitash had rarely been to the market. Going to school at night had left no time for browsing, and she had little money. This morning, she clutched the small purse with the forty birr her father had given her.

Daniel was worried. His eyes scouted for potential pick-pockets. "I don't want us to get robbed. And I surely don't want to get arrested by soldiers or security police who might be here looking for me."

Daniel's need to escape was never far from Alitash's mind. But now, holding his hand tightly, she allowed herself to savor the sights and sounds of the market, hardly knowing where to look first.

The market was the great heart of the city. And its color was brown.

Small clusters of Christian and Moslem peasants in brown tattered rags made little camps on the brown earth floor carpeted with dried twigs and stones, and strewn with animal and human refuse. The faces too were shades of brown and black, from copper-brown, like Alitash's, to café au lait to café noir and ebony.

Many of the women were startlingly beautiful, with aquiline noses, thin lips, and slender, graceful bodies. Young women walked like dancers, balancing on their heads heavy baskets of vegetables or dung, the dung to be used at home for fuel. The long hauls from the mountains to the market kept their bodies free of fat, and hunger and poverty took their toll.

Fires blazed on the ground as families cooked their food. Women in ragged burlap dresses nursed their babies. Naked children raced across the mud and gravel, indifferent to the flies and insects glued to their eyes. Some of their eyes were already white and sightless with trachoma.

Nineteen eighty was no famine year; heavy rains had helped end the periodic drought. But beggars were everywhere as

Alitash and Daniel moved through the little encampments until they reached the cattle area. Alitash saw a few cows and goats grazing, chickens were pecking at food inside bamboo cages, and four donkeys were for sale. Daniel examined the donkeys, opened their mouths, tapped their teeth, and selected a young one with huge doleful eyes and short sturdy legs.

"How much?" he asked the owner. Alitash watched excitedly as the game of buying and selling began.

"Sixty birr," the owner said.

Daniel pretended outrage. "Twenty birr. That's all we'll pay."

This time the owner acted outraged. "Twenty birr! Look at his legs. Look at his teeth. A prime donkey. Fifty-five birr."

Daniel shook his head. "Twenty-five."

"Fifty."

"Thirty."

"Forty-five."

"Thirty-five."

They finally compromised at forty birr. Without this play-acting, everyone would have been unhappy, the owner suspecting he had sold his donkey for too little, Daniel and Alitash fearing they had paid too much. Now everyone smiled.

While Alitash looked around to make sure no one knew how much money they were carrying, Daniel reached into his jeans to pay.

The proud owners of a reluctant donkey, they now had status. People looked at them differently, as if they were the children of wealth. Leather-faced old men and gaunt women accosted them with their hands outstretched. A barefoot man with pants cut above his knees and a tattered brown shamma offered to sell them one of the eight live chickens dangling from his shoulders.

Alitash handed Daniel her little purse. "You take the money," she said. "From now on, whatever we have will belong to both of us."

Daniel smiled at her, his cheeks dimpled with pleasure. Carefully, he slipped the purse into his jeans.

In the grain market, he bargained for fifty kilos of flour, and loaded the sacks on the donkey's back. To stave off suspicion, he mentioned casually they were buying grain for most of the village. In a pharmacist's shop, they bought medicines, and then moved on to the leather and rubber area. They stopped at a little stall with rows of sandals made of leather or strips of rubber tires. Alitash tried on a pair of leather sandals, bargained and bought them for five birr.

"Wear them now," Daniel said. "They look so good on your feet."

Alitash shook her head. "They're for the trip." She held them against her body and continued walking barefoot.

"I'm going to buy you a present—with my money," Daniel said.

"But you said I mustn't take anything—only what I wear."

"This is to wear."

He led her to the cloth and clothing area where dresses hung on poles outside tin-walled kiosks, and where bare-legged merchants sat on platforms surrounded by great bolts of woven cotton.

He selected a transparent white shamma with a delicate border of green and blue threads shot through with gold, and smiled again as Alitash draped it in Grecian-like folds around her body.

He stood back to admire her. "You are beautiful," he said.

Then, leading the donkeys, they walked back up the hills to Weleka, hurrying to reach home before noon to bathe in the river at the edge of the village, and prepare for the Sabbath.

The river was their social hall, their community center, and their *mikvah*, the ceremonial bath of physical and religious purification. They bathed so frequently that Christians called them "the people who smell of water."

Cleanliness was a ritual; during menstruation, women separated themselves from their families and moved into a menstrual hut, a small tukul set apart from the rest of the village with a semicircular barrier of stones. It was called the "shelter of curse" or the "shelter of blood." For the women, it was a welcome time, a time to rest from their labors. Some felt like queens, as relatives brought them their food and set it down inside the barrier of stones.

After their period was over, they returned to the river, washed their clothes and immersed themselves completely in the water. Clean once again, they could return home and sleep with their husbands.

A woman going into labor returned to the "shelter of blood." If she gave birth to a son, she remained in the hut for eight days, and fourteen days if she bore a daughter. Then, with her baby, she moved into the "maternity hut," and stayed there until she had spent forty days with her newborn son, or eighty days with her little daughter.

Generation after generation, they had held fast to their Jewishness through this ritual immersion and prayer. "Praise to the most high God . . . for Thou art the crown of the pure."

FIRST DANIEL joined the men scrupulously scrubbing their bodies while they talked and jested. When the men finished their ablutions, Alitash went down to the riverbank, chatting and laughing with the women and girls who now had the river to themselves. She washed her hair, her face, her ears, and let the cool, clean water flow over her firm breasts and her satin-smooth body. She smiled innocently, admiring her reflection in the water.

Then she changed into a fresh white dress which she had embroidered with Stars of David, and returned home.

"It was such an exciting time in the market," she said, trying to break through her mother's crust of anger.

Adalech's head was lowered.

"And Daniel bought me a new shamma. Look, Mother."

Adalech busied herself stirring the pot over the open fire.

"Mother, you think I'm running away. I'm not. Going to Israel is not running away. You know how dangerous it is to stay here."

"Don't talk to me about the dangers. You're leaving," Adalech blurted out. "Whatever you call it, you're leaving us. You're leaving me."

Alitash saw her mother's red-rimmed eyes. "You think I love Daniel more than I love you. I love you both."

"You're going to a strange land. Who do you know there? What kind of life will you have? Day and night I will worry."

Adalech's tears fell into the cooking vessel.

"Mother, please."

"Let's not talk anymore." Adalech whisked her hand across her cheek. "The Sabbath is coming."

ALL SATURDAY Alitash and her family rested.

No one cooked on the Sabbath. No one drew water from the river. No one worked in the fields or wove cloth or forged metal tools and knives. No one carved pottery or made a fire. Sex was forbidden, and even circumcisions were postponed until Sunday if the eighth day, biblically prescribed for circumcision, was the Sabbath.

Their religion was based on the Five Books of Moses. Fervently, they celebrated the holidays defined in the Torah—Rosh Hashanah, the Jewish New Year, and Yom Kippur, the Day of Atonement.

Passover especially had special meaning, for they identified themselves with the Jews who had been slaves in Egypt.

But, detached for centuries from the evolving Jewish religion, they knew nothing of talmudic traditions. Thus they did not observe the holidays that had evolved after the Five Books of Moses were recorded, holidays like Hannukah, the Festival of Freedom, and Purim, the joyous celebration of the beautiful Jewish queen in ancient Persia who had saved her people from Haman's destruction. Yet they knew the story, and celebrated it, not as Purim, but as the Fast of Esther.

Many of their customs were unknown to Jews in the rest of the world. Their spiritual leader was not a rabbi, but a *kess*— a priest. They had monks and, until the nineteenth century, were convinced all Jews were black and they were the only Jews left on earth.

They had even created their own holidays. The most unique was the Seged, a day of pilgrimage and prayer to celebrate the return of the Jews from the Babylonian exile.

On the Seged in late November, hundreds of people, often walking two or three days, climbed in a single line to the top of selected mountains.

The *kessoch*, dressed in ceremonial white shammas and white turbans, some shading themselves with embroidered and sequined umbrellas, opened the Bible, written in the ancient Ethiopic language of Ge'ez, to show the Law to the people.

All through the day, they prayed and fasted and read the Bible until, in the afternoon, they returned to their villages, ending the fast with a great feast, singing and dancing Ethiopian-style.

Now ON THE Sabbath morning, Alitash and her family went to the synagogue, where Kess Abebe stood at a cloth-decked table in front of the Ark. He was a small, slender man with a small face and a narrow black beard, dressed in a spotless white shamma and a white turban. Unlike many of the priests, he had studied Hebrew, and now he conducted the service, not as most did, in Ge'ez, but in modern Sephardic Hebrew.

The men and boys who knew Hebrew prayed with him; whenever he lifted the Torah out of the Ark, the women, sitting on the ledge encircling the wall, ululated with joy, making high-pitched rhythmic sounds as they rolled their tongues back and forth on the roofs of their mouths.

But Alitash scarcely listened. Sitting with her family against the mud wall, she stared at her father whose wisdom she cherished, and her mother whose delicate face seemed crumpled with unhappiness. She looked down at her pretty eight-year-old sister sitting beside her, and her two younger brothers. She wanted to press their features into her brain.

The realization of what she was giving up made her ache with guilt. She was leaving a village-bound world of quiet, gentle people who talked in low voices, of children who loved and honored their parents, and parents who, whether they were literate or not, taught their children to be kind and thoughtful and helpful to others, to walk humbly and worship the God of Abraham, Isaac, and Jacob.

They had suffered for their religion. For hundreds of years, they had been called "Falashas." "Falasha" meant "landless" and had come to mean "foreigner," "outcast," "stranger." And as strangers, they were easy victims of superstition and prejudice.

To many of the ignorant and illiterate among their Christian neighbors, they were *buda*—people of the evil eye.

The Christians believed that each night the Jews turned into hyenas—the dread scavengers with the bodies of foxes and the snouts of pigs, who hunted their prey in the darkness and drank the blood of Christian children.

If illness hit a family, the Jewish *buda* was to blame. If a peasant's cow or ox disappeared, a Falasha had turned himself into a *buda* and murdered the animal.

With new self-awareness, strengthened by their ties with Israel, the Jews insisted that the name Falasha be obliterated forever. They called themselves Beta Israel—"the House of Israel." Or simply, Ethiopian Jews.

All this—all that was painful in Weleka and all that was good, Alitash thought—all of it she was leaving behind forever.

RAIN FELL HEAVILY Shabbat afternoon, pounding on the tin roofs, and then stopped as suddenly as it had begun.

As dusk ended the Shabbat, the twenty young men and

women assembled in a coffeehouse in Gondar. Careful lest they be detected and reported to Major Malaku's men, they pretended they were having a *tej* party. *Tej* is the native drink made of fermented honey.

There was a fixed order to a *tej* party. First they drank the liquor from little bottles, talking quietly, and then began the coffee ritual which Alitash loved. While the others watched, she washed the coffee beans, roasted them on a metal sheet over the open fire of a little stove, ground them in a wooden pot with a metal pestle, boiled them on the same metal sheet three separate times, then, with the delicious aroma filling the house, served it in little cups.

In most *tej* parties, a singer would now stand up, drape her shamma seductively around her body, dance around the room, shaking her shoulders, tapping her foot, composing extemporaneous poems about the guests. But tonight no one sang or danced or recited poetry.

Daniel stood up, walked to the door, looked out carefully, then, convinced no one was outside who could hear him, returned to the group.

"I have had news of my teacher, Joseph," he said in a low voice.

"Joseph!" Alitash whispered. "Is he alive? Is he dead?"

"He is alive. He sent someone who had been in prison with him to tell me."

The young people moved closer on the mud floor; a candle threw a little circle of light on their faces. Alitash had met Daniel's teacher; she remembered his kindly dark eyes and ready smile. She had heard how, as a fourteen-year-old, he had been chosen to go to a school in Israel, had returned to Ethiopia in 1957, and had become a teacher in the government school in Ambober. At twenty, in Ethiopian tradition, he had married thirteen-year-old Hannah, one of his pupils, a shy youngster with round black eyes that seemed to sop up everything he could teach her.

In six years, Hannah had borne him four sons and a daughter, and then announced she wanted to finish school in Ambober. Joseph was astonished but agreed. Maybe one day Hannah too would be a teacher. But now they were living in Teda, where Joseph was headmaster of the village school. Some nights, too tired to walk three hours back to Teda, Hannah stayed with relatives in Ambober, while her sister helped Joseph take care of the children.

Alitash leaned forward, listening intently as Daniel began the story of his teacher's arrest. The rain had begun again, beating on the corrugated tin roof. "This is how Joseph's former prison mate told me the story," Daniel said.

IT WAS FOUR o'clock in the morning. Joseph and the children were awakened by a pounding on the door. Hannah was in Ambober. Three uniformed security police with guns knocked down the door. The children screamed. "What does this mean?" Joseph asked the security men. "What are you doing here?"

"You're under arrest," they said. "Orders from Major Malaku."

"What have I done?" Joseph asked.

"That's for you to tell the interrogator."

They put an iron chain around his wrists and tightened the chain with screws so they drew blood. Then they dragged him outside. There were soldiers and security police all around his house. They threw him into one of their Land-Rovers and drove him to Gondar. Here they pulled him out of the car in front of some kind of big wooden shack. They pushed him through the dirt courtyard. There were men lying on the ground with faces broken and smeared with blood. Some looked dead; some were moaning. Joseph could not believe that such things might be done to him.

They threw him into a dark room about twelve feet long. They locked the door. He was left alone, lying on a dirt and dung floor all stained with blood. The only things he saw in the room were two stands of iron about a foot and a half apart.

Time passed. Finally, a security policeman with a revolver on his hip and two big strong men who looked like thugs came into the room.

"Stand up," the man with the gun yelled.

Joseph pulled himself up. It was hard with his hands bound together and hurting.

"You have to tell us everything you did."

"I have nothing to tell you. I am a teacher. That's what I do. I teach children."

"You are a spy. You are spying for America and Israel, and you're smuggling your people out."

"It's not true," Joseph said.

"Confess," the man with the gun said. "Confess or we'll show you what we can do."

"I have nothing to confess. If you don't believe me, why don't you shoot me? You have a gun."

THE RAIN AND the pelting on the corrugated-iron roof had stopped. Daniel walked to the door, opened it, and looked out. A rush of mountain air burst into the coffeehouse. The little village lay in blackness. Convinced no one was outside, Daniel closed the door carefully. The candle lit up the anguished faces of the young people.

"Do you want more coffee?" Alitash asked him.

"Yes, thank you. Meanwhile I will go on. I will tell you the things Joseph's companion in the prison said while they still burn inside of me."

He sipped coffee from the little cup Alitash placed before him, and continued.

THE MAN WITH the gun gave a signal to the two men who looked like thugs. They tied Joseph's feet together with rope, dragged him to the two iron stands, and ordered him to crouch between them, holding his bound hands around his knees. Then they put a wooden stick under his knees, flipped him upside down, and placed the stick into the iron stands. While he hung this way, upside down, with his head touching the floor and his feet at their level, they took a rag and mopped the dirt floor with it. They pushed part of the rag into his mouth, deep into his throat so he thought he would suffocate. They pulled the ends of the rag tight around his face and tied them together so tight the blood ran from his mouth.

ALITASH CLAMPED her hands to her ears, but she could not stop herself from listening.

THEN THE MEN took two sticks of heavy rough wood with sharp corners like the unfinished legs of a table. They began to beat Joseph on the feet until the skin fell away and the bones were broken. Joseph saw his own blood spill on the floor. After a while he was unconscious. He did not know how long the beating went on. He woke to find himself lying in the dirt courtyard with the other prisoners.

He was tossed into a truck and taken to the Gondar prison. A prisoner put water in his mouth. He kept fainting all through the day. The next morning, police guards took him to the Gondar hospital. He heard a Russian doctor arguing with one of the policemen. "Are you playing with your brother? Do you know what you did to him? You could have killed him."

The Russian doctor tried to help Joseph, but the policeman slapped Joseph in the face and took him out of the hospital. In the truck, he drove him back to the torture room. Again the man with the gun appeared. "Why have you sold your country? Why are you smuggling Jews out of Ethiopia?"

Joseph couldn't talk. This time the two strong men put a rope under his armpits. His legs were too broken to hold the stick between them. Again they hung him upside down and beat him on his torn feet. After some fifteen minutes, he fainted. When he woke up, he found himself in Gondar prison, in one of the prison huts. The next day, his wife Hannah came to the prison to feed him or he would have starved to death.

"Is he alive now?" Alitash, sitting next to Daniel, whispered.

Daniel sighed as though he were dredging the story up from his guts. "The man he sent to me told me he's still in that prison, with three more teachers from Ambober. They were all my teachers—Yakov, Shlomo, Eli. Major Malaku got their names when he ordered the schools in the Jewish villages to bring him a list of all the students and all the teachers and their salaries."

"You see," Malka turned to Alitash, "we're all in danger."

Daniel seemed not to hear. He talked now like a man possessed. "The police broke into the houses of the three teachers, overturned everything. They said, 'We're looking for guns, papers, letters, documents. Where do you hide them?' When they found nothing, they destroyed the teachers' diplomas and certificates. They took the teachers to the same torture chamber where they had tortured Joseph. They asked similar questions: 'Why are you spying for Israel and the CIA? Why are you smuggling Jews out of Ethiopia?' They tortured them the same way, the beating on the feet until they fainted."

Tears rolled down Alitash's face. "And these three teachers—are they alive?" she asked.

"So far, yes," Daniel answered.

THE RAIN BEGAN again, like a steady drumbeat on the tin roof. Alitash pulled her shamma tightly around her.

They spoke now of what lay ahead. Daniel would, of course, be the leader, with his two best friends, Shmuel and Uri, as his chief lieutenants.

"We'll walk for a few days toward the Semien Mountains," Daniel said. "We'll get to a Jewish village in the hills where three men will join us. They will be our guides."

"You know them?" Malka asked.

"No."

"You trust them?"

"Yes."

"You trust people you don't know?" she demanded.

"There's no alternative. I don't know the way to Sudan. Uri doesn't. Shmuel doesn't. None of us do. Without guides, we'd get lost in the mountains."

"That's what my mother keeps worrying about," Alitash said. "She's afraid we'll never get there alive."

She stood up restlessly.

"I don't know which is worse," she said, her voice barely audible, as if she were thinking aloud. "If we stay, Major Malaku arrests Daniel, then maybe arrests all of us, and the torture—"

"That's why we have to leave fast," Malka interrupted.

"If we get out all right and he learns we're missing, he arrests our parents."

"I don't think I can go with you." A fifteen-year-old boy walked to the door. "I can't put my parents' lives in such danger from Major Malaku. I can't do it."

"Stay a while," Daniel said. "We pray to God Malaku won't discover we're gone. But fear mustn't stop us. Think of what we leave behind. No more *buda*. No more Falasha. No more being shot for the crime of going to high school."

The boy returned to the circle.

Daniel lit a new candle and looked at his friends, whose eyes were riveted on him. "This land we live in, it's not a land for Jews. Somewhere else there's a land for Jews. That's the land we must go to. Not from fear of torture but because it's our land. It's there, up there in Jerusalem. God told us we must live there. That's the promise he made to Abraham and Isaac and Jacob. I can picture it. The land will be greener than here; the animals will be healthier; the barley will grow taller. Like the Psalms say, we'll be lying down in green pastures."

He flung his arms out. "It's the Promised Land. There we'll be able to live free. Free as Jews."

IN THE PREDAWN hours of Sunday morning, a torrent of rain hammered a deafening tune on the roof of Alitash's house.

She walked to her mother and put her arms around her. They kissed each other's cheeks, their heads moving rapidly, Ethiopian-fashion, from one cheek to the other. Ordinarily, they would have kissed eight or ten times. Now after two kisses they stopped. Alitash could taste her mother's bitterness.

Then she and her father kissed each other's cheeks ten times. Her father swallowed hard, and whispered, "Go with God." Her brothers hugged her, but her little sister clung desperately to her legs. "Alitash, don't go. I won't let you go."

She bent down, lifted her sister, and held her tightly. The family watched as she walked out the door.

THE NIGHT WAS still black as the little group assembled in front of Daniel's house. In silence, they lashed their food and supplies on the back of the donkey and slipped out of the village.

"We must stay close together," Daniel whispered.

There were no roads, only paths made by mules and horses, and even the paths had disappeared with the rains.

The rain stopped as they climbed the gentle foothills, heading toward the Semien Mountains, rising above them in a wildly beautiful landscape. The sun began its ascent across the African sky, when Alitash heard a flock of brown wattled ibis with white patches mocking them raucously, "Haa-haa-haa." Black ravens swooped near them searching for food.

Darting abruptly out of a cave, a Walia ibex, a mammoth wild goat that weighed over two hundred pounds, with curved long horns, stopped to stare at them, then turned almost shyly and disappeared into the crags.

Finding a creek with fresh water, they stopped briefly to feed the donkey and to eat injera. Daniel gave each one a fistful of soup almonds made of wheat. "We'll save the rest of the almonds," he said. "We'll need them if we run out of food. With soup almonds and water," he explained, "you can make a whole meal." They continued climbing.

Midafternoon, they came upon a family of giant gelada baboons sitting on the edge of a cliff, their heads and bodies covered in thick fur cloaks, their chests almost obscenely naked with triangles of bright red skin. A tall male baboon turned his sad face toward them.

"Look at them." Alitash stared in wonder. "They're not afraid of us, so we're not afraid of them."

"I've heard they don't mind visitors by day. But at night, watch out. They don't want to be disturbed. People tell me they throw rocks at anybody who bothers them once they've gone to sleep."

NIGHT FALLS swiftly in the mountains.

The light had long been pulled from the sky when they reached their first target. Daniel knew the village, a small Jewish settlement with tukuls and a square of eucalyptus trees rimming the village like a fence. Here they would meet their guides.

Seeing neither candlelight nor oil lamps glowing inside the low doors, and unwilling to awaken the villagers, they unloaded the sacks from the donkey, wrapped themselves in their shammas against the cold mountain air, and bedded down on the earth floor.

Alitash was exhausted. But she could not sleep. Would Major Malaku carry out his threat to their parents? Had all twenty of them put their parents' lives at risk? Climbing the hills, she had been able to suppress these fears. Now they beat against her brain.

Pictures of her father planting vegetables in the tiny patch of land behind their house flashed through her head; she saw her mother fashioning little Queens of Sheba and King Solomons in little clay beds. She heard the happy sounds of her sister and her brothers playing. She began to tremble, visioning Major Malaku in his black boots and black leather jacket and his black riding whip racing his jeep into Weleka.

She tossed restlessly on the ground until she made herself believe her mother's arms were wrapped around her, and fell asleep.

Chapter Three

ALITASH AWOKE THE next morning to see the sun stroke the edges of the mountains pink and mauve. The villagers stepped out of their tukuls and welcomed the little group.

"I am Getachew," a dark-skinned young man with kinky hair and a commanding manner introduced himself. "I will be your guide with two others." Two young men stepped forward. All had the long legs of runners.

"We invite you into our huts for injera and coffee," Getachew said.

The group dispersed into different tukuls. The sunlit morning, the hospitable villagers, and the hot coffee revived Alitash's spirits.

Getachew called the group together and led them to an open space in the village.

"Today and tomorrow, we head north toward the Semien Mountains. We will be walking for several hundred kilometers."

Several hundred kilometers! Alitash glanced nervously at Daniel. He was listening intently as Getachew went on.

"We go west, then cross the border into Sudan. We have to get to a Sudanese refugee camp called Um Raquba. From there, we have to make our way to a town called Gedaref. In Gedaref, people will help you get to Jerusalem. That's where we leave you."

"After you leave us!" Malka shook her head. "In Sudan, we know no language, no people."

"Israelis will find you."

"But how?"

"I'm not sure. But they will meet you. They will take you to Israel. You will get there, believe me."

His exhortation to believe him made Alitash uneasy.

"How long do you think it will take?" Daniel asked.

"Hard to tell. Three weeks. A month. Maybe more. A lot depends on the rain. I see by your donkey and supplies you're well prepared. That's good."

The guides had to be paid in advance. Daniel gave Getachew thirty birr. He would have to husband the remaining money carefully.

The men loaded the food and supplies in side packs on the donkey and thanked the villagers who wished them Godspeed and safety.

Getachew was in the vanguard, pressing ahead, allowing no time to rest the donkey or themselves. The sun beat down on them. Alitash's lips were parched.

Long past noon, Getachew called out, "There's a spring a few kilometers from here. That's where we'll make our first stop."

Then she saw it—a little stream of water glistening with stabs of golden sunlight.

She raced toward it, bent down, and scooped the cold, clean water into her mouth. Daniel and Shmuel led the overheated donkey to the water, and soon everyone was down at the stream, washing and drinking and preparing to break bread. Then they stretched out on the ground.

Alitash rested beside Daniel. She spoke softly so that no one but Daniel could hear her. "Getachew, and the other two guides, they're like no people I ever met. They hardly talk."

"They know all the dangers."

"Then why do they risk themselves for strangers like us? Is it for the money?"

Daniel shook his head. "It's not for money. They give up other work to do this."

"Then why?"

"Because they believe. That's their main reason. They want to help people like us get to Jerusalem. Then someday they'll come too."

"You're sure he knows where he's taking us?"

"Yes. He knows these hills well."

Alitash looked across the reclining group at Getachew. "He's taken others before us?"

"We're the first group going this way."

"But we know nothing about him. His family, his village, what he does when he's not with us."

"That's the way it must be," Daniel said. "People who risk their lives have to be faceless."

Getachew rose. "Time to go. We must be prepared now. We will meet people, peasants mostly. Remember, they do not often see strangers. Sometimes they will see us as friendly. And sometimes they will see us as enemies. We must be very careful. All the time."

Late afternoon, they caught sight of a green square hedge of olive and cedar trees rising almost vertically on the side of a hill. Over the hedge, they could see the straw roofs of tukuls topped by a small round building. It was the church.

"Wait behind this cliff," Getachew ordered. "I'll scout around the village. If there are any soldiers or police, we turn around and disappear."

"It's a friendly settlement," Getachew reported. "I told them we were Christian students on vacation. They've invited us to spend the night."

Inside the village, they introduced themselves with false names and talked politely of their supposed outing. Knowing the poverty of the villages and the overcrowded tukuls, they assured the highlanders they had brought their own food and needed no shelter.

They unloaded the donkey, and, a little distance from the tukuls, built an outdoor fire on which Alitash and the four other girls cooked their supper. Hungrily, they placed the cold injera as a base on their plates, then tore off pieces of the pancakes and dipped them into the spicy, sizzling *wot.*

Darkness settled like a taut drum over the village. They stretched their tired bodies on the ground and slept.

Alitash was awakened in the middle of the night by a cold rain. She wrapped her arms around herself, went back to sleep, and woke the next morning in a pool of water. She stood up, brushing the water from her arms, wringing it from her clothes. The rain had stopped, and the sun, already rising, soon dried her.

The little group breakfasted, loaded the donkey, and set out toward the Semien Mountains. Once again, in the clean gold light of Africa, Alitash was a happy, outgoing fifteen-year-old embarking on the great adventure of her life.

"I'm so glad I've come." She squeezed Daniel's hand, feeling his warmth and strength.

Ahead of them, the white shammas of their friends seemed to sail like billowing clouds in the wind.

"Tell me again what you think we'll do in Israel?" she asked. "I love to hear you tell it."

40

"We'll finish school. Both of us. I want to work in electricity. Maybe I can be an engineer."

"An engineer in Israel," she said, slowly, as if she were hearing it for the first time. "And I can become a teacher. I can teach children to read and write and draw pictures and— I can even teach them the things my mother taught me. Tell me more."

"When we finish studying, we'll marry, and have children. And wherever we settle, we'll make pilgrimages to Jerusalem."

Jerusalem. She shut her eyes for a moment. She could almost touch the hills, golden with sunset, that she had seen in picture books.

"We'll climb the Holy Mountain," she said as the Semiens loomed above them, the highest mountains in Ethiopia, whose peaks soared fifteen thousand feet above the sea.

THEY WERE encircled in an awesome landscape of cliffs and plunging canyons, of purple and green escarpments rising often needle-sharp against the turquoise sky.

For long stretches they met no people as they climbed single file up the jagged cliffs, holding on to branches and scrambling over treacherous narrow ledges.

The days began to run into each other. Walking. Eating. Searching for water. Building fires. Cooking the food they had brought with them. Trying, whenever they could, to spend their nights in the Jewish settlements perched on the side, and even on top, of the cliffs.

Centuries ago, the Jews had fled to these nearly inaccessible mountains, sometimes the better to fight their enemies, other times to escape persecution from Christian rulers who demanded, "Convert or die." Their history was shrouded in a mist of exotic tales. How had they come to this corner of a black African country whose name, given it by the ancient Greeks, meant "the land of the burnt faces"? Were they really descendants of the famous night of love between the beautiful Queen of Sheba and King Solomon, the wise king who reigned over Israel from about 961 to 922 B.C. and who had amassed a thousand wives and concubines?

Historians, anthropologists, social scientists, rabbis had their own theories.

In 1973, the Sephardic chief rabbi of Israel, Ovadia Yosef, concluded that the Jews of Ethiopia were descendants of the Lost Tribe of Dan.

Others claimed they were converts, brought into Judaism by Yemenite Jews who traveled to Ethiopia across the Red Sea.

Some believed they were led here by Moses, who had married an Ethiopian woman when he was sent by Pharaoh to conquer Ethiopia.

Still others were sure they were descendants of Jews who fled from Israel after the destruction of the First Temple, settled in a community called Elephantine in Upper Egypt, and then migrated to Ethiopia, where they established a Jewish kingdom with Jewish kings and queens.

In Ethiopia itself, the romantic story of King Solomon and the Queen was the national legend. Did not Haile Selassie, who called himself the Lion of Judah, claim he was a direct descendant of King Solomon? Proof, the Ethiopians said, was in the Bible, in the First Book of the Kings:

And when the queen of Sheba heard of the fame of Solomon concerning the name of the Lord, she came to prove him with hard questions. And she came to Jerusalem with a very great train, with camels that bore spices, and very much gold, and precious stones. . . . And Solomon told her all her questions. . . . And she said to the king, . . . Howbeit I believed not the words, until I came, and mine eyes had seen it, and behold, the half was not told me: thy wisdom and prosperity exceedeth the fame which I heard. . . . Blessed be Jehovah thy God, who delighteth in

*thee, to set thee on the throne of Israel: because Jehovah
loved Israel forever. . . . And King Solomon gave unto the
Queen of Sheba all her desire. . . . So she turned and went
to her country, she and her servants.*

Alitash had read the story of how *Solomon gave unto the
Queen of Sheba all her desire.*

THE LEGEND continued beyond the biblical account. Returning to Ethiopia, the Queen, now converted to Judaism,
gave birth to a son whom she named Menelik, meaning "son
of the wise man."

A few years later, she sent Menelik to Jerusalem to be reared
by his father as a Jewish prince. Solomon raised him with
love and care, and then, in the tradition of the dynasties of
the time, returned him to his mother with a bodyguard of the
most precious of the children of Israel—the first-born sons of
his courtiers and warriors—who then married the Queen's
handmaidens.

Of this version of the legend, the more educated and sophisticated Jews believed only the portion in the Book of
the Kings.

The Christian version that Alitash learned in school was
different.

The story begins the same way. The Queen of Sheba, who
now has a name, Makeda, travels with her entourage and
gifts to the land of Israel to meet the wise Jewish king. Solomon
is smitten with her beauty and invites her to his bed. She
refuses. Solomon makes a pact with her. If she will touch
nothing in the palace, he will not put a hand upon her. She
agrees.

But the night before she is to leave, Solomon prepares a
banquet to honor her. He orders his cooks to make the meal
hot and spicy. After the banquet, Makeda, driven by thirst
and unable to sleep, comes out of her bedroom, and, finding

water, drinks it eagerly. She has broken the pact. Solomon draws her into his bedroom and seduces her.

Returning to Ethiopia, Makeda gives birth to Menelik who, as a lad of thirteen, asks the Queen who his father is. She reveals he is the son of the king of the Jews, and sends him to Jerusalem to meet his father. Handsome and wise, Menelik becomes his father's favorite. After several years, jealous courtiers, fearing he will inherit Solomon's throne, prevail on the king to send him back to his mother.

Solomon does so reluctantly. But he commands his courtiers to send their first-born sons with Menelik. He crowns Menelik king of Ethiopia, and, as a farewell gift, Solomon prepares a copy of the sacred Ark of the Covenant which God had given Moses on Mount Sinai.

Menelik is to take the copy back to Ethiopia. Instead, he and his priests decide to outwit Solomon and steal the true Ark. They replace it in Jerusalem with the copy, and bring the original to Aksum, the ancient capital of Ethiopia near the Red Sea.

To this day, the Christians believe the story so firmly that each year on the festival of Epiphany, the priests of the Ethiopian Orthodox Church take Moses' "original" Ark with its Ten Commandments out of the Holy of Holies in the cathedral at Aksum. And on the seventh day of each month, the Day of the Holy Trinity, copies of the Tablets, enshrined in some of the forty-four thousand churches, are shown to the believers.

Despite the intertwining of legend and history, most historians agree that two thousand years ago Judaism was the dominant faith in Ethiopia. A million Jews were believed to have lived here, even winning over the Agaus, one of the tribes in the ancient Aksum Empire. In the fourth century, the emperor was converted and Christianity became the prevailing religion, only to be threatened three hundred years later by the Moslems whose armies swept across Africa into Ethiopia.

The Jews, caught in the religious wars between the Christians and Moslems, took refuge in the mountains, where they set up the first independent Jewish kingdom after the destruction of Jerusalem in A.D. 70.

In the tenth century, a Jewish queen named Judith was believed to have sacked Aksum, the Ethiopian capital, and ruled for forty years. After Judith's overthrow, the Jews continued to live on top of the mountains, fighting their enemies and clinging fiercely to their faith. They were the country's blacksmiths and ironmongers, forging lances and shields for their own and other warring armies.

But their very skill with fire had its drawbacks; the Christians looked upon them as sorcerers practicing black magic. Hence the charge that Jews were *buda*—people of the evil eye.

The arrival of the Portuguese, searching for new lands to conquer in the sixteenth century, marked the end of Jewish fighting power. The Catholic Portuguese armed the Ethiopian Christians with guns and cannon. The lances and shields of the Jews were no match for gunpowder.

The Jews were ordered again to convert or die. In 1577, a Christian emperor, Sarsa Dengel, began a policy of extermination. For seventeen years, the Jews held out in the Semien Mountains, hurling rocks and boulders to stop the march of the fully equipped soldiers. To prevent being captured, men cut each other's throats with spears and knives. Women and young girls, tied by their wrists to the invaders, jumped off the cliffs, pulling their persecutors with them. It was Massada, Ethiopian-style. On the ground, their heads were severed and brought to the king. The emperor's army scaled the heights, burned many of the villages, and massacred most of the survivors.

What was left of the Jewish kingdom was destroyed in the seventeenth century. Jews were no longer allowed to own land, they were persecuted, tormented, sold into slavery.

Isolated from the world, they were intermittently "rediscovered" by travelers and explorers. The most famous was the six-foot-four, redheaded Scotsman James Bruce, who spent two years, 1769 and 1770, in Gondar. "The Jews," he wrote admiringly, "still preserve the religion, language and manners of their ancestors."

"Rediscovered" again in the nineteenth century, the Jews became the special target of English missionaries. By the turn of the twentieth century, the Jewish population had been reduced to some ninety thousand.

Now in 1980, they were twenty-eight thousand, living in small isolated villages in the highlands.

It was to these Jewish villages that Getachew led the band of young people.

INSIDE THE JEWISH villages, the travelers told the truth—they were Jews on their way to Jerusalem. They talked so glowingly of their dreams that the villagers too began to dream. Maybe someday they too would leave their tukuls, come down from the mountains, trek to Sudan, and fly to the Holy City.

Seeing how eager the villagers were to learn more about the mystical Jewish land that lay north of Africa, Getachew occasionally allowed Alitash and Daniel and the group of young people to rest. "We can spend today and tomorrow here. Here we're safe." So safe that they even told the villagers their true names.

But in the Christian and Moslem villages, fearing they would be turned over to the soldier patrols, they manufactured so many different stories that often in the morning they forgot the version they had told the night before.

In one village, they said they were running away from home. The villagers eyed them with suspicion, but allowed them to spend the night sleeping outside the ring of tukuls. In another village, they said soldiers were chasing them because they were students, opposed to the Marxist government. Fortunately, this was a village whose people were opposed to the government. Their tukuls were too crowded to offer shelter, but they fed

the young people, and even gave them fresh injera and vegetables for their journey.

One night they saw smoke curling up in the distance. Bone-
tired, they let down their guard. Instead of sending someone
to scout the village, they walked directly toward it. They
stopped abruptly. Soldiers were at the entrance.

Alitash's heart pounded so hard she was afraid the soldiers
would hear it. She knew if the soldiers saw them, no questions would be asked. They would be shot for trying to flee
the country.

Then, like a small miracle, a sudden fog rose up from the
ground, so dense they could not see their hands before them.

Noiselessly, they turned around and hurried away.

Rain lashed them in torrential sheets and still they dared
not stop to find shelter. All night they walked, sinking almost
to their knees in mud.

Alitash's white dress and the white shamma Daniel had
bought her were weighted down with dirt and brackish brown
water. In the darkness, bushes and brambles tore her face and
bare legs.

It was early morning when they reached the Armachiho
Forest, and at last, concealing themselves among the trees,
they stretched out on the wet earth and slept.

THE DAYS IN the mountains were brutally hot. The nights
were wet and freezing cold, and the air was rife with the
disease-breeding insects of the tropics.

"We not only have to watch out for all kinds of bugs and
insects," Getachew said, "we've got to keep watch that poi-
sonous snakes don't attack us while we sleep."

For among the natural enemies they faced were snakes in
the forest, crocodiles who ate unwary fishermen and travelers, and microscopic worms that lived inside snails in the rivers, invaded the body through bare feet, and caused the dread
disease of bilharzia.

Each night, to protect themselves, they built platform beds of fallen trees. With no roofs over their heads, they woke each morning wet and cold.

EARLY ONE evening, a pride of lions emerged and stealthily followed them. The friendly baboons and the handsome ibex had intrigued Alitash. But lions! She clung to Daniel.

"What do we do?" she whispered.

"We just keep walking. I'm told they won't attack us unless we frighten them."

"But what if they're hungry?"

"We're in greater danger from people than from animals."

Daniel spoke the truth.

They hid whenever they saw a few men walking or riding mules. They were sure the men were bandit gangs, *shifta*, who roamed the mountains. Alitash had heard hair-raising stories of how they robbed anyone they caught, then killed the men, stripped women and even ten-year-old girls, and raped them. Jewish women were the most vulnerable. Alitash knew of Jewish women who tattooed crosses on their foreheads to pretend they were Christians.

Mekonnen, a fifteen-year-old who had come on the journey with his older brother, went to Daniel. "I can't take any more of this. *Shifta*. Lions. Soldiers. Snakes. I'm going back."

"You're out of your mind." Daniel and Mekonnen's brother tried to dissuade him. "We've come a long way. You're crazy to try to go back alone. You're in much greater danger alone than staying with us. We're a whole group. We can fight back. We can try to protect each other. If you're caught, you'll have nobody to protect you."

Makonnen would not listen. "I'll find my way. The rest of you are never going to get to Jerusalem. I don't know if you're going to live long enough even to get to Sudan."

48

Chapter Four

MEKONNEN'S DEPARTURE threw a pall over the group.
Two weeks had passed since they had left Weleka.
Their food was gone. In one of the settlements, they sold their
donkey. They tied the few supplies they had left with rope to
their backs. They bought food in friendly villages until their
money too gave out. Then they gathered mushrooms and ate
grass and leaves. Alitash had never been so hungry in her life.

Each night, before they dropped off to sleep, they made a
small arrow on a tree to show them the direction they had
come from. One morning they awoke and found the night
rain had washed the arrow away. They put up a new arrow
and began to walk.

There was great fear. They walked all that day, tired, worried. Everything looked the same—the blue sky on top, the mud on bottom. The long shadows of the trees were disappearing when they came upon the platform beds on which they had slept the night before. They had been walking in a circle.

Frustrated and exhausted, they fell asleep. The next morning, they set out again. After six hours of searching, they finally found the path Getachew was seeking.

They walked more cheerfully now.

"From now on, nothing can go wrong," Alitash said, clutching Daniel's hand.

Daniel's white teeth shone in his brown face. "I wouldn't be so sure. Wait 'til we reach Jerusalem."

Then he leaned over and kissed her.

Now THEY WERE deep inside the Armachiho Forest. Here bandits and murderers found refuge. Here warlords ruled over the scattered camps and settlements.

Late one afternoon, a half dozen men materialized from behind the trees. They ranged from boys barely in their teens to men in their fifties, all barelegged, some in old burlap shammas. Pointing their guns and knives, they surrounded the young people and demanded money.

"We have no money," Getachew spoke for the group. "Search us. We have nothing."

The men searched and found the young people had nothing but the little bundles of clothing on their backs.

A pock-faced man nudged Daniel with his rifle. "Our chief will decide what to do with you."

He herded the group to a small clearing with a sprinkling of straw tukuls and patches of poorly plowed land. A barelegged man with charcoal skin, black hooded eyes, and a scraggly black beard latticed with gray sat smoking a cigarette. He held a stick in his left hand.

"We searched them, Berhun." The pock-faced man spoke

50

first. "They have nothing. They will work if we give them food."

"Who are you?" The chief blew smoke through his nose.

Daniel answered. "We're students on vacation. We lost our way."

The chief narrowed his hooded eyes. "You look strong," he said.

There was a long pause. "If you work for us," the chief said, "we will give you food."

"Will we be paid as well?" Daniel asked.

"When you leave, we will pay."

"How much?"

"How much? How do I know how much until you have finished working."

The young people looked at each other. At least there would be food.

THE DAYS MOVED slowly, steadily. From early morning to dusk, Daniel, Getachew, and the boys worked in the fields, while Alitash and the four girls ground corn and *teff*, cooked the food, and made injera. Chief Berhun took most of the food; the young people ate what was left. Each night, sleeping in the field, the boys took turns guarding the girls.

A week passed when Getachew and Daniel appeared before the chief.

"We would like to leave now."

"I will tell you when you can go."

He waved his stick. One of his men stood by polishing his rifle. Another raised his gun.

Two weeks passed. Three weeks. A month.

"We're like slaves," Alitash said. "Maybe they will never let us go."

"It is like slavery," Daniel said. "But we'll find a way. At least here we have food. And when we leave, we'll have not only food but money."

They had been in the Armachiho Forest for nearly three

months when, on a Saturday afternoon, Daniel and Getachew slipped away from the group and their guards and walked
beyond the confines of the settlement. After a while, they
met a charcoal-skinned man carrying a rifle on his shoulder.

"You are strangers here," he said. "Who are you?"

"We are students."

"Students! What are students doing in the Armachiho
Forest?"

Daniel scanned the young man's face. Something familiar,
something tribal, made him blurt out, "We are not only students. We are Jews."

"Jews!" The stranger stepped back in wonder. "I too am a
Jew. *Sanbat salam.*"

"*Sanbat salam,*" Daniel replied, and then added in Hebrew,
"*Shabbat shalom.*"

The young man introduced himself. His name was Joshua.

Daniel and Getachew gave him their names. "Jews in the
forest!" Daniel said. "We never thought . . ."

Joshua nodded. "Not everybody in the forest is a bandit.
We have a little settlement not far from here. What brought
you to the forest?"

"We were trying to get to Sudan and Jerusalem when we—"

"Jews are going to Jerusalem?" Joshua interrupted.

"Some have already arrived. You have not heard?"

"Here in the forest we hear little. What have you been doing
here?"

"Working for Berhun and his people," Daniel said.

"Like slaves," Getachew added. "They stand with guns, so
we can't leave."

"How long?"

"Three months."

"You have women with you?"

"Five."

"They have not molested your women?" Joshua asked.

"We guard them well."

"When do you think to leave?"

"We ask to leave constantly," Daniel said. "The chief

threatens us. We can leave, he says, only when he permits it. Then he will pay us. We have no money."

"Can you be ready tomorrow?"

Daniel nodded.

"Say nothing until the morning. Then tell Berhun you are leaving and ask for your money. I will have others with me. We will conceal ourselves in the woods. If you need us, shout my name."

That night the boys stood guard more carefully than ever.

In the morning, strapping their little bundles of clothing on their backs, they presented themselves to Berhun.

"We are leaving today," Daniel said.

The chief lowered his hooded eyes in silence.

"How much will you pay us?" Daniel asked.

The chief rubbed his stick in the earth. "Twenty-five birr," he said at last.

"Twenty-five birr? Twenty-two people worked for you for three months!"

"Twenty-five birr."

Daniel looked at the little group. They knew they were trapped.

"We will take it."

The chief handed Daniel the money. "The men can go," he said. "The women stay with us."

The five girls moved close together. Daniel cupped his lips with his hands and shouted, "Joshua! Joshua! Joshua!"

A dozen men with rifles pointed raced into the camp. Daniel explained quickly. "They want our girls."

Joshua moved in front of the chief, his finger on his rifle. "If you keep those girls, we will take revenge on you."

The chief held his stick in the air nonchalantly, but his eyes looked wary. "What revenge?"

"You think we will tell you? You will suffer."

Alitash saw the chief lean back. His hooded eyes closed shut. "*Buda*"—she heard him hiss the word. For once she was grateful for the ugly superstition. Let him believe these young men would turn into hyenas and wreak revenge.

Berhun opened his eyes. "Give back the twenty-five birr and bring your clothes to me. You keep what you wear."

Daniel looked swiftly at Joshua, who shrugged his shoulders. Daniel handed the twenty-five birr to the chief, who still puffed his cigarette in silence. The young people dropped their little bundles and walked quickly out of the camp.

Joshua and his men stayed with them for a few hours, leading them through the forest. "Here we leave you. This path will take you to Sudan."

"You saved our girls," Daniel embraced him. "You saved our lives."

Joshua returned the embrace and prayed:

> *May God's Name be praised from the earth to the heavens.*
>
> *May God's Name be praised from the angels' encampment to the adobes of man.*
>
> *May God's Name be praised from the abyss of light to the abyss of darkness.*

"Thank the Lord God of Israel. He saved you," Joshua said, and walked back toward his settlement in the Armachiho Forest.

ALL THE NEXT day, the rain fell heavily. The following morning, they came to a river hurtling across rocks and boulders. Alitash, looking down at the water, was sure that with a single misstep they would be sucked down the raging stream.

While they stood trying to decide how best to navigate the rocks and water, a group of peasants came down to fish.

Daniel approached them. "How does one cross this river?"

The peasants smiled. "We will help you. We know this river well."

One by one, they hoisted each of the twenty-three young people on their backs, and going back and forth, maneuvered their way around the boulders to the opposite shore.

"We have nothing to give you," Daniel said. "We have no money, not even clothes."

"No matter. May you reach your goal in safety."

AND STILL THE hard African rain beat down on them as if they were being tested.

"We're getting close." Getachew tried to raise their spirits. But his own spirits were obviously low.

A few days later, they came to another river. They waited for hours, praying peasants would come again to fish. But no one came. They would have to find some way to get themselves across.

They found two trees that had been felled by lightning. The men lifted the first tree from the ground and heaved it across the gorge to the opposite bank. They threw the second tree a few feet higher than the first. Next they tied themselves to one another, knotting the rope around their waists and legs and hands, making a human bridge. The men were to go first. Daniel led the way, his feet on the lower tree, his hands holding onto the higher one, his body bent over, testing each step before he put his foot down. The men moved slowly behind him.

Then came the young women. Alitash was first.

She clung hard to the tree trunk, so hard she could feel the wood digging into her skin. She dared not look at the water raging below her.

Daniel called out, "Alitash, you're doing fine. You're almost here."

She felt his strong arms lifting her up the riverbank. She held her breath until the men lifted the four other girls out of the water, and now the whole group hugged and kissed and wept and laughed and continued the trek.

A WEEK passed. Ahead lay another forest stretching to the horizon. They walked for several days, ate berries and grasses, and slept fitfully, until at last they came to a wide, calm river.

"There it is!" Getachew shouted. "There, across the river, is Sudan!"

Sudan!

Alitash shaded her eyes, searching the land across the river. They would be out of Ethiopia. On the road to freedom.

But how to cross this last river?

On both banks, they saw no one.

For hours, Alitash sat forlornly on the riverbank, Daniel beside her. Her clothes were filthy. Her body, forever clamoring for food, felt loathsome. Was it possible no one would come?

Daniel too was depressed. "We've come this far," he said. "And now, who knows? Maybe we'll be caught like those twenty-eight—" He stopped.

Getachew had told them how in 1975 some twenty-eight strong young Jews had tried to escape through Kenya. The Jewish Agency in Jerusalem had worked out the plan, and even arranged for vehicles to move the young people from their villages in the Gondar Province to the border with Kenya.

But 1975 was a bad time for everyone in Ethiopia. The revolutionary government, which had taken power one year before, was purging scores of people. Murder was a ritual in the streets of Addis Ababa.

The twenty-eight young Jews made their way safely across Ethiopia. They reached the border. Just ahead of them they could see Kenya—and freedom—when Ethiopian border police found them. They were imprisoned, tortured, and sent back to their villages.

Daniel and Alitash left the group and walked dejectedly along the empty bank. Would they suffer the same fate?

THEY RETURNED TO their friends. Getachew was talking. "We must be very cautious. This is where we're in double danger. On this side, we can be caught by Ethiopian soldiers. If they catch us, and our luck holds, we'll be sent back to our homes. If our luck doesn't hold, we'll be killed. On the Sudan side"— he paused—"we can be caught too. I don't know what they'll do to us . . ."

Somewhere in the distance, Alitash heard birds calling.

There was a long silence. They were alone, isolated, facing danger on two sides of a muddy river.

THE DOUBLE DANGER rose from the intertwined history of two totally different lands. Ethiopia had some 40 million people and twenty-eight thousand Jews. Sudan, the largest country in Africa, had less than 10 million people and almost no Jews. Yet in the halls of the United Nations, the representatives of Sudan and Ethiopia, violently opposed to each other's governments, voted together consistently, religiously, adamantly, on one issue—hostility to Israel.

Ethiopia, a Soviet client, had an army of three hundred thousand men, the largest army in black Africa, with some two thousand Russian military advisors and nearly two thousand Cubans guarding the rebellious borders.

Sudan, part of the Arab world, was a partner in good standing of the Arab League. It was a quasi-democracy whose president, Gaafar Mohammed el-Nimeiri, ruled like a dictator.

Now both countries were in turmoil—Marxist Ethiopia trying to suppress dissident Marxist guerrillas trying to secede, Sudan trying to Moslemize its rebellious Christians. Each supported the other's rebellions.

Ironically, the guerrilla warfare, with the two neighboring countries in chaos, helped open a window for Christian and Moslem refugees to escape from Ethiopia to Sudan. But would it open a window for the Jews?

IT WAS GETACHEW who spotted them first—a patrol of Sudanese soldiers marching along the Sudanese border.

With the others, Alitash cupped her hands around her lips, shouting in the English she had learned in school, "Help! Help us!"

The soldiers heard the noise, raised their guns, and called across the river in Arab-accented English, "Who are you?

Getachew answered, "We're Ethiopian Christians. We're running away from the Communists. We ask asylum."

The soldiers shouted back: "We'll send a boat. Let three men come across. The rest wait where you are."

Daniel, Shmuel, and Uri volunteered. For two hours, the soldiers interrogated them. They tried to convince the soldiers that they were Orthodox Christian refugees fleeing the Marxist government. The soldiers were not convinced. Still, they sent a boat for the others, searched them, and found they had nothing but their tattered clothes and mud-soaked shammas.

"Until we find out who you really are, and what you're planning to do in Sudan," the soldiers said, "we're locking you up."

They led the group of young exhausted Jews to a military camp and imprisoned them in a cagelike hut secured with prison bars. The girls were locked in one cell of the hut, the boys in another. For food, they were given bread and a watery soup with rice.

Alitash had long hours to look back upon the trek. It had been a trek of hazards and fears and discoveries, a trek that brought her closer than ever to the people she loved, to Daniel and her friends. But it was also a a trek of self-discovery. Her childhood was over. She was Alitash, daughter of Adalech and Solomon, on her way to the Holy Land, and nothing would stop her.

To pass the time, the girls sang songs for the boys to hear, told stories, and, in the end, helped lift their own spirits.

Seven days and nights passed slowly. On the eighth day, two soldiers came to the girls' cell and held up a little mirror, a comb, and a small bar of soap. These were luxuries that

58

few villagers could afford. Even in Weleka, they saw their reflections only when they bathed naked in the river.

"Take them." The soldiers smiled. "Just a little present."

The girls were delighted. Alitash looked at herself in the mirror. The once-happy, outgoing fifteen-year-old looked ravaged. She burst into laughter. It was the first time she had laughed all week.

That night the two soldiers, reeking of alcohol, broke into the girls' cell. They grabbed Alitash and Yael and began tearing their clothes. The girls scratched their faces, fought the soldiers, and screamed for help.

Hearing them, the boys beat their hands against the prison bars. "Don't touch those girls," they yelled. "We'll kill you when we get out."

Two Sudanese officers, driving by, heard the commotion. They dashed into the prison hut and pulled the soldiers away.

"It's all right," they assured Alitash and Yael, who were still trembling in shock. "We'll make sure this doesn't happen again."

For punishment, the two soldiers were forced to stand that night in the cold and all the next day in the broiling sun, holding their rifles over their heads.

Daniel was angry. "Alitash," he called out, "promise you'll never accept anything again from strangers. And if we ever get out of here, promise you'll never go anywhere without one of us men beside you."

Alitash could still smell the soldier's drunken breath and feel his hands ripping her clothes. "Of course I promise."

She spent the rest of the day in silence. Through the prison bars, she watched the two soldiers, their arms sagging as they held their guns over their heads, their faces and tattered uniforms drenched with sweat.

The following day, the officers returned and unlocked the prison. They led the young people past clusters of soldiers with guns slung on their backs, to an open area in the military camp.

The older of the two men addressed them. "We had to convince ourselves that you were really Christian refugees before we could release you." He smiled benignly. "You've convinced us."

Alitash lowered her head. How different these men were from the ones who had burst into their cell. In these nine days in prison, she had met two kinds of Sudanese—good ones like these two men, and evil ones. Was that what the world outside Weleka was like? Good and evil?

The officer was still speaking. "We're going to send you to a refugee camp. It's called Um Raquba."

She gasped. Um Raquba! The refugee camp they were trying to reach!

The officer shouted an order to a sergeant. "Get a truck over here."

Soon a large army truck pulled up. A soldier with a gun on his back guarded them as they climbed in, then climbed up after them.

From being nearly raped to being sent to Um Raquba by truck! Not to have to trek all those miles. Good things could happen too.

THE UM RAQUBA they had longed to reach was a city of despair. Thousands of refugees milled listlessly around streets lined with tukuls and tents. Garbage was strewn in dirt alleyways, naked children ran wild, mothers nursing nearly naked babies sat apathetically in front of the tents and grass huts.

Still, for Alitash, the camp was a haven. Relief agencies from America and Canada and Europe were here, feeding the people. At last, she had water and soap, a day's ration of food and milk, and a place to sleep in the field.

For the next five days, they were interrogated by soldiers. The questioning, in a small straw hut, lasted from morning until night.

Your names? Again they gave false Christian names.

What did you do in Ethiopia? We were all students.

Why did you leave? We were in danger of being killed. Students are a special target.

How did you come here? We walked.

You walked, hundreds of kilometers? Yes, we walked.

Do you know any people in the camp? No.

How can we be sure you're not spies for the Ethiopian government? We're not spies. We just want asylum.

On the sixth day, one of the interrogators said, "You can stay for a while."

Now they had refugee status—bona fide Christian refugees. Now they could come to the area where food was parceled out and draw the meager rations that kept the refugees on the razor's edge just above starvation.

One day, browsing through the makeshift marketplace, they saw a family of Ethiopian Christians they knew from Gondar. They hurried away, hoping they had not been seen.

Another day they were ready to queue up for food when they heard three men boasting of their exploits as members of the EPRP—the Ethiopian People's Revolutionary Party—the extreme leftist rebel group. The EPRP had murdered a number of Jews for refusing to join the insurrection against the Marxist government. They slipped away from the queue. Better to be hungry than discovered.

The refugees hated the Jews with age-old prejudices, hated them for being *buda;* hated them because of the rumors that Jews could escape and reach Israel while they had no place to run.

From friendly refugees, they heard how, at night, men, drunk from *tej* and home-brewed beer, broke into the Jewish tents and tukuls in the camp, looting and stealing, knifing some, poisoning others, and raping the women.

"We have to get out of here fast," Getachew declared. "We must get to Gedaref."

Gedaref was where they would meet someone from Israel, someone who would take over. Gedaref was nearly a hundred

kilometers to the north. But how would they get there without being picked up by police?

They needed two things: money for a bus, and legitimate
documents permitting them to travel. They had neither.

Refugees in Um Raquba were allowed to work for Sudanese
farmers near the camp. The whole group went to work. They
plowed the land and planted seed and finally earned enough
money for bus fare.

To get twenty-two travel documents was more difficult. They
told the Sudanese camp authorities they needed to go to
Gedaref to buy decent clothing. The authorities could see their
clothes were in rags. Their shoes and sandals had long ago
worn out.

"We'll let three of you go," the authorities agreed. "You
can bring back clothes for the rest." They gave them three
permits to travel.

It was decided that Getachew and the two other guides
should make the trip. In Gedaref, Getachew would try to meet
the unknown Israeli, and then figure out a way to bring the
others.

But there were no buses. The heavy rains had made the
road impassable. Only trucks or Land-Rovers could navigate
the water-clogged highway.

Daniel went back to the farmers and found one who owned
a truck. In a mixture of the little Arabic he had picked up
working in the Sudanese fields, some English, and much hand
language, Daniel struck a deal. The farmer agreed to take some
of their bus fare money and drive them all to Gedaref. This
was far better than sending the three guides by bus. That night
the little group huddled together working out their strategy.

The next morning, in drenching rain, the three guides walked
to the camp entrance. It was a makeshift gate of two stumps
of trees with a wall of straw and twigs. They showed their
travel permits to the soldiers, who waved them out. They
climbed onto the truck standing outside the gate entrance,
drove a mile up the road, and waited.

One by one, the others slipped out of an opening on the side of the camp, reached the road, and moved stealthily until they rendezvoused with the men in the truck. Crouching out of sight on the truck floor, they took off, confident that at last they were out of danger.

But the rains kept falling. The road became even more rutted. The truck broke down.

The farmer walked away with their money. They were stranded.

In panic, they scouted the terrain and discovered they were near a village. With no options, they entered the village and, to their great relief, found the villagers friendly. The people took them into their homes and placed before them a pail of water, a pail of camel's milk, and some meat.

Gratefully, they swallowed the water in large gulps. But, despite their hunger and thirst, they did not touch the camel's milk or the meat. The camel's milk and the meat were not kosher.

The next day, the villagers helped them find another farmer who owned a tractor and a wagon. He agreed, for a fee, to take them to Gedaref. But his wagon, tied umbilically to his tractor, could hold only ten people on its wooden floor.

They decided that the farmer should take the five young women and five of the men, leave them at a designated spot in the marketplace in Gedaref, and return for the others. As a precaution, they told the farmer the five couples were husbands and wives. Married women were less likely to be raped.

The rain stopped at last. Relentlessly, the desert sun beat down on the wagon slumping forward on the mud road. Alitash shut her eyes and slept.

Three hours later, they reached Gedaref, a small dusty market town, with square houses made of sun-baked brick, flat roofs, and narrow windows to keep out the sun. The day was furnace-hot.

The farmer selected a spot near the entrance to the marketplace, unloaded the passengers, and promised to return with the others.

"We have to make ourselves as inconspicuous as possible," Getachew warned.

Inconspicuous! Alitash looked at the villagers, holiday-clean in flowing white cotton clothes, the men in white jellabas and white turbans, the women wrapped from head to toe in long, spotless white gowns. Alitash had never felt so filthy and forlorn.

Every soldier was a threat. Every policeman looked threatening. She smelled the food that farmers were selling, she could almost taste it. But all their money was gone.

And where was Daniel? What delayed him? Her mind conjured up a parade of disasters. Soldiers had arrested him. He was being tortured, hung by his feet, with soldiers beating his feet with sticks, like Major Malaku's bastinado. The wagon had broken down on the rutted road. The men were walking; it would take days to reach Gedaref. She pictured them dying of thirst and starvation and sunstroke.

Late in the afternoon, the truck pulled up before them. Alitash raced toward Daniel as he jumped to the ground. They kissed, their heads swinging rapidly, six times, eight times, ten times, cheek-to-cheek. She clung to his body.

"Let's go," Getachew said. "We have to find a place to sleep."

Still trying to look inconspicuous, they left the market and walked along an unpaved street. A sign in Amharic on a low building told them they had found a small inn run by Ethiopians.

The owners, a black middle-aged couple with white curly hair, greeted them warmly, led them to a bare dormitory room with a row of ten narrow beds lining the wall, brought water and fresh fruit, and showed them where to shower and even wash their clothes.

Alitash had never seen a shower, but once she learned its mysteries, she soaped her body from her hair to her callused feet, shutting her eyes with pleasure as she turned and twisted under the stream of water beating down on her.

It was the first time since they had left Weleka that she felt clean.

THE WHITEWASHED walls were cracking; old window shutters hid them from the outside world. Alitash and Malka and a few of the others stretched out on the narrow beds, the rest sat on the floor. Once again they were waiting.

"How safe are we here?" Malka voiced their concern to Getachew.

"How safe can Jews be in an Arab land?" Getachew answered. "Still, someone from Israel should be coming around pretty soon."

"How will they know we're here?" Daniel asked.

"They have their sources."

The hotel owners brought them food and asked no questions. Were these kindly middle-aged people the sources? Alitash wondered.

The first day passed, and no one came.

"How much longer do you think?" Daniel again queried Getachew.

"No idea."

"Days? Weeks? How long?"

"I don't know."

"Cooped up in this room?"

"We've come this far. We can't risk going out on the street and being picked up by the Sudanese police."

The second evening, a small wiry man in faded jeans and a white shirt knocked on their door. A mustache and narrow black beard rimmed his lips and chin. His eyes sparkled like black ball bearings. He looked like a Jewish prince in jeans.

"You made it," he exclaimed. "Thank God you made it."

He walked around the room shaking their hands, hugging them, then kissing their cheeks back and forth. Alitash felt as if she had been lost and this wiry young man had found her.

He spoke in clipped sentences. "Don't ask me my real name. Call me Emanuel. The less you know about me the better.

This much I can tell you. I'm an Ethiopian Jew. Israel is my home, but I go back and forth to Sudan and Ethiopia. You mustn't ask me how. I'll pay your bill, so you don't have to worry about money here in Sudan."

He looked around the dormitory room at the young people sitting on the edge of the beds and on the floor. "I want to hear about your trip."

They took turns describing the close encounter with the soldiers, the lions in the mountains, the dangers in the Armachiho Forest, the river crossings, the close call with rape in the prison cell in Sudan, and finally the escape from Um Raquba with only three permits.

Emanuel's eyes grew moist as he heard their adventures. "You made it. You made it this far. That's what counts. Now others will make it too. I can see them coming, groups like yours, bigger ones even. It's starting. The exodus is starting."

He walked around the hotel room, hugging some of the boys, patting others on the back, smiling and nodding at the girls. "We must get everybody out. No more torture. No more imprisonment. We'll get all our people into Israel."

He was saying the words they had dared not even dream. *We'll get all our people into Israel.* They sprang up from the floor and the beds, embracing each other.

"Now wait a minute," he cautioned. "We still have to get you out of Sudan. We can run into real trouble."

His manner changed. "First of all, we have to get you passports. We'll need passport pictures. I wish you could look like members of one family."

"Why?" several asked at the same time.

"Then we can get group passports. Families get out of the country easier than a lot of strong young people."

He surveyed the hotel bedroom. The girls were fifteen and sixteen; the boys a little older. Daniel at eighteen was one of the oldest.

"Besides, you're all unrelated. We would have to get each of you an individual passport. That would take a long time."

He sat down at the edge of one of the beds. "We'll have to wait for more refugees to arrive. We hope some will come with older parents, and some with children. Then we can put families together of different ages and take pictures."

"How long could that be?" Alitash asked.

Emanuel shrugged his shoulders. "It's in the hands of God."

But what if no families came? Could old people and little children make the trek? How long could they hole up in this little inn? Alitash's excitement at Emanuel's words began to turn into despair.

"Even after we get you passports," Emanuel said, "we still have to get you exit permits to leave Sudan, and visas to enter Europe."

"And that will take . . . ?"

"That too is in God's hands." He walked toward the door. "I have to go now. I'll be back first thing tomorrow morning."

Getachew stopped him.

"I'm leaving in the morning. I'm going back to Ethiopia."

Emanuel shook his hand and kissed him, cheek-to-cheek. "Now you know the way. Bring more Jews out. We want to save them all."

He handed Getachew a purse with Ethiopian birr and Sudanese pounds. Then he was gone, as mysteriously and swiftly as he had first appeared.

The young people settled themselves on the edges of the beds and on the floor. The bare hotel room seemed emptier than ever.

"I don't know Emanuel's real name," Getachew said, "but I can tell you this—he is a man of the Mossad, Israel's intelligence agency. They risk their lives every day to save our people."

"WE MUST SEPARATE you," Emanuel announced the next morning. "It's too dangerous to have all of you together. If the police come around, checking, there'll be real trouble. I'm going to divide you into two houses where you'll be safe."

While Emanuel left to pay the innkeepers, the group bade farewell to Getachew, each one kissing him three times.

"I will see all your families," Getachew promised, "and tell them how you are. Some day, God willing, I too will get to Jerusalem."

Emanuel returned in time to say good-bye to Getachew. Then he selected four young people. "You'll be the first group," he said. He turned to the others, who looked apprehensive. "I'm not abandoning you. I'll keep coming back."

Carefully, looking up and down the street, he led the group out of the inn and, true to his word, kept returning until early afternoon. Alitash and Daniel insisted on being last.

Heat seemed to rise from the bowels of the earth as they walked through the dusty town, glancing furtively to make sure they were not followed. In a quiet neighborhood, they walked past a small mosque and entered a low flat-topped brick house, one of a row of similar houses.

A tall, ebony-skinned Sudanese woman in a white robe opened the door and hurried them in. Yael and Shmuel, who had fallen in love during the trek, were waiting for them.

"You must not go out on the street," Emanuel warned. "You must not be seen even at a window. A single wrong move, and—" He stopped. "Everything you've come through could be wiped out. We can be all thrown into jail."

"What do we do now?" Daniel asked.

"Nothing. Except wait."

Wait. Wait. Wait. Alitash bit her lips. The patience she had learned in Weleka was wearing thin.

"Tonight," Emanuel said, "I will move in here to be with you. One of my friends will move into the second safe house. We'll bring you food and some clothes. From now on, you'll see me only at night."

Alitash learned that, during the day, Emanuel and his friends worked as unskilled laborers in homes and farms. This was their cover. At night they worked saving Jews. They seemed never to sleep.

DAY AFTER DAY, the young people waited, cooped up in the small brick house. They could walk freely through the sparsely furnished rooms, but the windows were shuttered, the door was shut.

Several times Alitash caught herself eyeing the door. If only she could walk out for a few moments. If only she could get a quick respite from the grueling heat.

"Don't try," Daniel warned. "It's too dangerous."

The house came to life at night when Emanuel returned. He was their link with the outside world. He brought them fresh food, news of Israel, and especially news of Ethiopia. An international organization called "Amnesty International," he told them, had issued a report with terrible details of imprisonment in Ethiopia and torture.

Cautiously, he read them a section of the November 1978 report. "Alleged methods of torture include: dipping the body in hot oil and splashing hot oil on the face; raping of women, including young girls; inserting a bottle or heated iron bar into the vagina or anus; tying of a bottle of water to the testicles; pulling-out of the nails of fingers and toes." He put the report down. "I can't read any more."

Alitash put her face in her hands. Fear for her parents washed over her. Was she murdering them by making this journey?

"DO THE SUDANESE leaders know about us?" Daniel asked Emanuel one evening.

"Some do, of course. We couldn't operate without them."

The long trek had taught Daniel some of the basics of life-saving. "Do you have to pay them a lot?"

Emanuel searched Daniel's face as if he were trying to decide how much he could reveal.

"We pay some, yes. Everything costs money—especially this kind of work. But basically, Sudan is a decent country, with very decent people. Many help us without any compensation—just because they're good human beings."

"And the government. Does it help too?"

Again Emanuel looked at the group. "You ask many questions; I will answer whatever I can. When I don't answer, it's because some things cannot be told. The rulers of Sudan, President Nimeiri, walks a tightrope between the Arab countries and the countries of the West. He's the only Arab leader who recognized the Camp David peace treaty between Israel and Egypt."

"A peace treaty!" Daniel stared at Emanuel, unbelieving.

"Yes. It was signed in America."

"We never heard anything about a peace treaty. In school, all we heard was how Russia and Cuba and the Arab states hate Israel. They don't even call it Israel. They call it the name Major Malaku calls it, 'the Zionist entity,' and day and night they plan how to destroy it."

Emanuel lit a cigarette. "The important thing about this treaty is that it's with Egypt. Without Egypt, other Arab countries won't fight Israel. Egypt makes war and Egypt makes peace. Egypt started four wars against Israel, and lost all of them. The country you're going to may finally have . . ." He paused, and then spoke the word "peace" as if he were caressing it.

"And Sudan?" Malka asked. "Is there peace with Sudan?"

"Sudan was never at war with Israel."

He blew smoke through his nose. "Nimeiri is in a rough spot. He's close to Egypt's President Anwar Sadat. He'd like to get closer to the United States. At the same time, Arab countries have lots of foreign agents here, spying on him and on one another. That's why we have to be so careful."

The room grew heavy with smoke and apprehension.

"And that's one of the reasons why, even when you get to Israel, you must not tell anyone the route you took."

He lowered his voice. "Don't even breathe the word 'Sudan.' "

"THEY'VE COME," Emanuel shouted as he shut the door behind him. It was two weeks since they had moved into the safe house.

"It's a miracle. Four groups of refugees—twenty people—have come into Gedaref."

They crowded around him. "Families?"

"Yes. Grandparents. Young fathers and mothers. Little children, two and three and four. Young mothers with babies on their backs."

Alitash broke through the crowd. "Any from our villages?" Maybe there was word of her family.

"No. They've come all the way from Tigray and they're exhausted."

Tigray was the province east of Gondar, where the Jews were caught in the crossfire between the Ethiopian government and the rebels trying to secede.

"They walked hundreds and hundreds of kilometers," Emanuel said. "Two old people and a child died on the way. They buried them under stones."

He paused, his face clouded.

"I'll bring them here tomorrow morning. Now that they've come, things should move fast."

The next morning, twenty Tigrayans, led by Emanuel, slipped furtively into the safe house. Their shammas were tattered and filthy, their faces were drawn with hunger, their dark eyes were hooded with refugee fear. They look, Alitash thought, the way we looked a few weeks ago.

Gently, she and Yael showed the women and little children how to use the shower, then Daniel and Shmuel helped the men.

At noon, Emanuel came back with a photographer who posed the people into four "family" groups. Alitash and Daniel became part of one family group, Malka and Yael and Shmuel part of another.

A few days later, Emanuel opened his bag and took out four brand-new booklets.

"Passports," he said. "These are your passports."

One by one, they studied the passports in wonder.

That night Emanuel led them out of the safe house and helped them climb up into a truck. "Get down on the floor," he whispered. "We don't want to be stopped by police."

Alitash's stomach churned. So, even with passports, they were still in danger. When would it end?

At four in the morning, they arrived at a house somewhere near an airstrip. It stood alone in a field, against the black sky.

They entered to find it packed tightly with people. Alitash rushed toward her friends who had arrived earlier from the second safe house. They hugged and kissed one another as if they had been separated not for two weeks but for months.

Again Emanuel whispered first in Amharic and then in the words of Tigrinya that he knew, "You must be absolutely silent. Anyone who happens to walk by outside must not even suspect you're here."

The house, hot with bodies crushed against each other, became ghostly still. People scarcely talked to one another; when they did, they had to concentrate to hear. Anyone near a child who seemed about to whimper clapped his hand on the child's mouth. If a baby cried, its mother pushed her breast into the baby's mouth. Soon even the babies seemed to sense they must not make a sound.

Every few hours, Emanuel returned, sometimes with food, other times with clean clothes for the ragged travelers. Each time, he whispered before he departed, "Not yet."

The windows of the house were kept tightly shut.

Much of the day Alitash spent sitting on the floor, squeezed between Daniel and Malka. Once she fell asleep for a few minutes, and then woke with a start. She had dreamt she was back in the quiet of Weleka. Dazed, she looked around at the people pressed against the walls. Where was she? Who were all these people? And why was this room so stifling hot?

She decided to take a cold shower. But as soon as she stepped back into her clothes, the heat enveloped her like wet steam. An hour later, she took a second shower. Then a third. There was no relief.

At dusk, a white-bearded man motioned to the people on the floor to move back a few inches. Then other men rose and wrapped their shammas around their heads and bodies. Moving only their lips, they sang the evening prayers.

Alitash moved her lips with them. "Dear God," she murmured. "We're so close now. Please get us there safely."

Darkness descended. The people made little groups on the floor, some with their heads touching other people's toes, some holding a child in each arm. They tried to sleep.

THE SUN HAD not yet risen on the fourth morning when Emanuel tiptoed through the little camps of sleepers, quietly rousing the people. "We're going on foot to the airport. Follow me."

Quickly, they picked themselves up from the floor, carried their children, and followed him. They had no baggage to delay them.

They hurried along a dirt road, heading for the airstrip. They met no one. Alitash, running to keep up with Daniel, saw the plane in the distance, shining silver in the rising sun. Could that plane take them up in the air? She continued running until Emanuel halted the march.

He motioned to Daniel to come close. "From here on, you are the leader."

He handed Daniel the precious passports and waved farewell to the people.

"This is where I leave you. The police mustn't know that I'm with you."

"What will happen to you?" Daniel asked.

Emanuel's black eyes crinkled mischievously. "I'll see you in Israel."

Daniel led the people to a small hangar. Soldiers, guarding it with guns, demanded to see the passports. Daniel held them up like flags.

The soldiers motioned for him to enter quickly, followed by the others, who moved in fear and bewilderment.

Daniel stood at a table solemnly watching an official check the photos and then the faces of the "families." Satisfied, the official stamped the passports. Customs was perfunctory. They had nothing to declare.

A soldier stood guard at the exit door as the still terrified refugees hurried onto the airstrip.

"Look at it," a man near Alitash shouted. "It's a big bird!"

Alitash felt blood rush to her head. The plane stood alone against the rising sun, like something holy. The man was right. With outstretched wings, it was like the mythical birds in the ancient legends, the birds that flew kings and emperors to fabled lands. The bird that would fly them out of Africa, out of the Middle Ages, out of persecution and danger to freedom.

She waited on the ground until Daniel had helped all the refugees aboard, then she climbed the stairs and found a seat. Daniel took the seat beside her.

The day was already hot, the plane even hotter, but Alitash hardly noticed.

A flight attendant walked down the aisles helping the people fasten their seat belts. Alitash heard the sound of the engines as they revved up. The plane was off, gliding gently then roaring as it left the ground and flew into the sky.

She stared out the window. The parched land began to recede. Thoughts of her family in Weleka raced through her head. Would she ever see them again? A wave of homesickness swept over her. Tears rolled down her cheeks. Daniel put his arm around her.

"It will be all right," he said, and gently wiped the tears from her cheeks.

ATHENS. The airport. A stranger approached Daniel and whispered something in Hebrew.

Daniel handed him the passports and the man vanished.

The refugees huddled together in the airport, waiting, watching, until another stranger approached and, with a nod of his head, motioned to them to follow him. They entered a bus and were taken to a hotel for the night.

The next morning, they were handed brand-new Israeli passports and driven back to the airport. Another "big bird" waited to engulf them. But this one, glistening in the morning sun, was blue and white, the colors of Israel, and on its body was the Star of David and the words "El Al."

Alitash sat upright in her seat, less afraid. She stroked the new passport, still unbelieving. She was legal. A legal Jew with a legal passport flying to the Promised Land.

The plane banked and flew into the sky, over Europe, across the blue-green Mediterranean, then low over the white stone buildings of Tel Aviv, and landed.

Tears ran down Alitash's cheeks.

"*Shalom, shalom,*" a young Jew called out as the people descended. "*Baruch haba* [Blessed be your coming]."

They were led inside the airport, where they were given hot coffee and sandwiches and fruit.

"Do you know what day this is?" Daniel asked Alitash.

She shook her head.

"I've just learned," he said. "It's Rosh Hashanah."

The Jewish New Year had just begun.

Chapter Five

I N THE FALL of 1979, Yona ben Naftali attempted to leave.

Yona was the spokesman for the Jews of the Gondar region.

Living in Addis Ababa, he was their representative in dealing with government officials, their ambassador in welcoming visitors who came from other lands.

Like Alitash, Yona was born in Weleka. And like Daniel, Yona was under surveillance.

He was a courtly man with skin the color of freshly ground coffee. A white mustache framed his lips and a small white beard traveled fan-shape around his brown chin.

He could have been a Jewish scholar in New York, or the

76

principal of a high school. In fact, he had been the head of all the Jewish schools in Ethiopia, supported by money from the Jewish Agency in Jerusalem and later with money from American and European Jews.

He had reached one of the highest positions held by a Jew in the Haile Selassie regime. He was the director of the Translation Department in the Ministry of Education. Gifted in seven languages, he had translated the *Pirkei Avot* (Sayings of the Fathers) from Hebrew into Amharic. He had compiled a Hebrew-Amharic dictionary. He had published an Amharic book explaining the Jewish holidays and festivals.

One evening a Christian friend, Gebreyesus, came surreptitiously to his home, a modest wooden house made of mud walls set back in a bare courtyard. His neighbors were government workers and small tradesmen.

"Yona," his friend warned. "I hear rumors that the police are onto you."

Yona was silent. He knew that the security people in Addis Ababa had good reason. Since the mid-1970s, when the secret exodus began, he had helped many of the young people starting out on the hazardous trek. The exodus was still a trickle, but a few hundred had already reached Israel.

"I don't know just when they plan to arrest you," Gebreyesus said. "But I suggest you start making plans to get out of the country."

His friend slipped out of the house.

Yona knew he had to get out. But how? Alitash and Daniel's group had fled on foot across the mountains and desert. But Alitash was fifteen. Yona was seventy-two and asthmatic.

He sat silently on the settee in the living room. Despite his difficulty in breathing, he carried himself tall and straight, a man who had known power.

He looked across the coffee table at his wife. It was nearly forty years since he had fallen in love with Tourou, fourteen years younger than he, whose name meant "beautiful." Now, still stately and handsome, she was a matronly woman with dark olive skin, high cheekbones, and worldly-wise, almond-shaped eyes that gave her a kind of Eurasian beauty.

A night breeze whistling through the lace curtains made her draw her white shamma around her shoulders. Dressed in a white silk dress with blue polka dots, a blue turban around her hair, and gold sandals on her dark stockingless feet, she would have looked at home in an apartment in Geneva or New York.

In the tradition of Ethiopia, she had kept her own name after she married Yona. There are no family names in Ethiopia. A child is given its own first name, the second name is the name of its father. Her father's name was Abraham, so she was Tourou Abraham, and each of her eight children, with biblical names like Judith, David, and Jeremiah, became Judith Yona, David Yona, and Jeremiah Yona.

Tourou talked proudly to her children of her grandfather, an artisan who had been forceably taken from his village in the mountains around Gondar and transported, with other skilled Jews, to Addis Ababa to work for Emperor Menelik II. Few Ethiopians knew that the Jews had built most of the fine edifices in Menelik's new capital city.

"Don't ever forget," Tourou told her children, "that it was your great-grandfather who helped build the emperor's National Palace and the Church of Holy Mary."

But the capital, Addis Ababa, a nearly all-Christian city, was a difficult place for Jews to practice their Judaism. The bodies of Jews who died in Addis were frequently sent back to the villages around Gondar to be given a Jewish burial.

Despite the difficulties, Tourou was proud that her grandfather, then her father, and now she and Yona and their children had clung fiercely to their faith. She had borne her eight children as a blessing from God, and, like all Ethiopian women, she had cooked and sewn and woven brilliantly colored tablebaskets shaped like Romanesque domes. But unlike most women of her generation, Tourou could read and write Amharic.

"We must find a way to get out quickly," Yona said.

Tourou bit her lips. "You go alone," she said. "It will be easier for you to get a passport if you go alone. I will remain behind and be your guarantor."

Anyone permitted out of Ethiopia had to leave a guarantor—a man or woman who guaranteed that the traveler would return at a specified time. If the traveler did not return then, the guarantor could be arrested, fined thousands of birr, imprisoned for years, even killed.

"My guarantor!" Yona exploded. "What if I don't come back? You could be arrested and—" He stopped himself from saying the dread word, "killed."

"I'm not the one in trouble," Tourou said. "You are."

"I won't leave without you. I need you. When my asthma attacks come and I can't breathe, you're there to help. And you," his dark eyes softened with compassion, "even though you can give yourself those shots—you need me too."

Tourou Abraham was a diabetic. Each day she injected herself with insulin, a drug hard to come by in Ethiopia. Often, weakened by her disease, she took to her bed for two or three weeks.

Laboriously, she raised herself in her chair. "Yona, you didn't listen to what I said. *You're* in danger. Not me."

Determined to upset neither her nor himself, he walked out of the house and settled himself on the front wooden stairs. He struggled to inhale great drafts of air to break the pain and congestion in his lungs.

Ruefully, he thought of his long separations from Tourou and the children. He had spent weeks at a time traveling through the northern provinces of Gondar and Tigray, inspecting the Jewish schools, secretly garnering intelligence on how the Jews were faring.

He closed his eyes, remembering the packed buses and the "Gondar taxis," the ancient horses and primitive wagons that had taken him up and down the winding paths to the Jewish villages.

He could see himself again, riding mules or scrambling on foot up the fortresslike mountains where for centuries the black Jews had taken refuge from their enemies.

He knew those mountain villages like the lines in his hands. He had spent more than three decades sitting in little classrooms with children whose small dark faces and huge dark eyes seemed to hunger for learning, entering their tukuls and mud huts, breaking injera bread with their elders, listening to their problems, trying desperately to help.

He could measure his life in successes and failures. He could dole out the $30,000 a year sent him by the Falasha Welfare Association in England, a few American supporters, and by the Jewish Agency in Jerusalem to pay the paltry salaries the teachers earned. He could give the pupils pens and notebooks too costly for most Ethiopian children to buy. But that for which the young people yearned—to go to Israel—that for which he himself now yearned, for that he had to find ways as dangerous as breaking out of prison.

Restlessly, he stood up and walked to the tin fence, thinking of the incongruities in the lives of Ethiopians.

Educated Christians had fewer difficulties than Jews in getting passports. They had viable excuses. Some said they wanted to visit the Christian Orthodox Church in Jerusalem. Others said they wanted to continue their education in Paris or London, in New York or Los Angeles; then they would return with graduate degrees and help educate other Ethiopians. Many were allowed to go, provided they had guarantors. Occasionally, even Jewish students were given permission to study abroad, provided they too had guarantors and promised to return.

But Yona was no student.

He looked up at the blue African sky circling like a bowl around the dark city. He could see lights in his neighbors' houses. But the daytime noises of horses and carts clattering down the dirt road outside his fence were silenced.

The usual crowds of people, talking, arguing, buying and

selling home-grown tropical fruits and vegetables, queueing up for rations at government stores, were nowhere in sight.

Addis was under strict curfew, a nightly reminder that Ethiopia was at war. War with its own rebels and guerrillas, war with the secessionists who wanted independence.

Only with the curfew could Comrade Mengistu Haile Mariam, general secretary of the Central Committee (CC) of the Workers' Party of Ethiopia (WPE), chairman of the Provisional Military Administrative Council (PMAC), commander-in-chief of the Revolutionary Armed Forces, hope to control the country.

The country was in chaos.

On the right, in what became known as the "White Terror," were the followers of Haile Selassie and the landlords who had lost some of their land, despised the Communist regime, and formed the EDU—the Ethiopian Democratic Union.

On the extreme left were the rebels fighting a long-drawn-out civil war in the northern provinces of Eritrea and Tigray. They were Marxists opposing their Marxist government, trying to secede from Ethiopia and create their own nation. In the rebel areas, there were villages controlled by the government by day. The night belonged to the guerrillas.

Caught in the center were the Jews, scapegoats of the White Terror landlords who enslaved them as sharecroppers, and the guerrillas who denounced them as "Zionist imperialists."

INSIDE HIS courtyard, Yona was safe from the soldiers policing the street, enforcing the nine o'clock curfew. Around him, the city lay dark and silent, like a sleeping beast.

With a million people, Addis Ababa shut itself down with a threatening silence that ran along the empty streets, blacking out the government buildings and palaces and churches, obscuring the modernistic center for the Organization of African Unity, the OAU, immobilizing the Mercato, the largest outdoor market in Africa, where during the day hordes of people pressed against one another in narrow bazaars and shops and music stores that sent the rhythmic staccato Ethiopian music blaring through the turmoil. The Mercato now was empty and heavily bolted.

Darkness and the eerie silence enveloped even the vast empty concrete piazza called Revolution Square, which featured bigger than life-size color posters of the Communist triumvirate—Marx, Engels, and Lenin—and a gigantic poster of Lieutenant Colonel Mengistu.

Only a few military and police cars drove along Addis' longest street. The government had changed many names, but not this one. It was still called Churchill Boulevard in honor of the British who had liberated Ethiopia from the Italians in World War II.

The people of Addis were now inside their homes, some in luxurious villas surrounded by fences and gardens with lush tropical flowers and trees; others in sleek modern apartment houses with radios and television sets; but most in shacks along the main road or squeezed into festering alleys and tin-roofed shantytowns with no indoor plumbing, and water from one community spigot.

Addis Ababa had one foot in the twentieth century and one foot in the eleventh.

On the streets were bundles of rags that occasionally moved. Inside the rags were people. The homeless. The dispossessed, sleeping in front of both the villas and the shacks.

For Addis, the Marxist socialist capital, was a mixture of wealth rubbing shoulders with poverty, of capitalism in bed with communism. Most housing was nationalized, banking was nationalized, industries were nationalized. But merchants could own their own shops, and make as much profit as the market would bear.

YONA PACED THE courtyard thinking of his children, five of whom were already in Israel.

His heart pounded as he remembered how close Jeremiah had been to death. Jeremiah, his sixth child, had been caught in the May Day massacre in 1977 that had killed two thousand high school and university students.

The two years since the massacre peeled away in his memory. He felt the pain in his lungs again, reliving the horror.

Jeremiah, then eighteen, had been teaching in an elementary school in the Gondar area, when he took a few days off to come to Addis.

At six in the morning, security police jumped out of jeeps and trucks, and with guns blazing, burst into the homes in Yona's neighborhood. Anyone who looked like a student was dragged out of his bed.

Tourou screamed as Jeremiah was thrown into a police truck and driven off to prison. Jeremiah found himself behind bars with twenty-three of his friends.

Yona and Tourou flung on their clothes and rushed to the police station. Tears streamed down Tourou's face. "My son has done nothing," she wept. "He came for only a few days to see us. He's not a student, he's a teacher."

In the Ethiopian revolution, students were the enemy. High school and university students were the ones who demonstrated and caused trouble. Teachers, paid by the government, were more likely to be silent.

"I have proof he's not a student," Yona pleaded. "Here, this shows he's a teacher."

Yona drew out of his pocket a list of teachers and their salaries; Jeremiah's name was on the list.

Yona never learned whether it was Tourou's tears that worked, or the list of teachers, or the stroke of luck that a rigidly Marxist and hostile police supervisor was out of his office, and his young assistant believed them.

At one o'clock, the assistant set Jeremiah free, warning him to go into hiding. If the supervisor saw him, he would be arrested again and killed.

Jeremiah's twenty-three friends were less fortunate. They were taken to the woods and shot.

For five months, Jeremiah hid from the police in a relative's house near the airport.

YONA RETURNED indoors. Tourou was waiting for him.

"Have you decided?" she asked him.

"I won't go alone."

"You're risking your life."

"I'll write to the children in Israel. Maybe they'll find a way to get us out together."

Yona wrote a cautious letter to his son, thirty-year-old David, who lived in Petah Tikva near Tel Aviv.

David was in every way Yona's son, with sparkling black eyes, a black mustache, and a small black beard framing his chin. After completing three years at Haile Selassie University in Addis Ababa, David decided he wanted freedom in Israel and in 1971 Yona had agreed that he should go.

Yona's friend, Professor Norman Bentwich, the British scholar, arranged a scholarship at the Hebrew University in Jerusalem. David was given a passport with the understanding that he would return to Ethiopia and become a teacher.

Instead, he became an Israeli. In 1975, he married Raquel, a nurse whom he had met in Addis, and the following year entered the Israeli army. He rose to the rank of sergeant and became a missile-weapons surveyor. Joining the handful of Ethiopians in Israel, he was elected secretary of the activist Association of Ethiopian Jews in Israel.

Understanding the urgency in Yona's letter, David rushed to Jerusalem to see a friend in the Ministry of Foreign Affairs.

"Write a letter to the Ethiopian government," his friend suggested, "and ask them to let your father leave. Then take the letter to the head of the Ethiopian church in Jerusalem and ask him to sign it. He has influence in Addis. If he agrees,

84

bring the letter back here and I will forward it myself to the Ethiopian government in Addis Ababa."

The Ethiopian Orthodox Church was on Rehov Hahabashim—the Street of the Ethiopians—in the center of Jerusalem. David was granted an audience with the religious leader. "I can't sign your letter," he told David regretfully. "It would put me in danger, and it would not be good for your family."

Dejected, David returned to the Foreign Ministry.

"Where do we go from here?" he asked his friend.

"We'll enlist the help of Rabbi Moses Rosen. He's the chief rabbi of Romania. Romania and Ethiopia are both Communist countries. Ethiopia might do something for him."

Rabbi Rosen agreed to help. He sent a letter directly to Addis, addressed to "Yona ben Naftali, President of the Jewish Community of Ethiopia."

Yona received the letter and instantly destroyed it. He was no president, nor was there an organized Jewish community. Bringing such a letter to the Communist authorities would make him more suspect than ever.

Every avenue of escape seemed closed. David refused to give up. One morning he appeared at a printer's shop. "I want you to print a single wedding invitation," he said. "In Hebrew and in English. Make it fancy, with designs around it."

David sent the single invitation to Addis inviting Yona and Tourou to the "wedding" of their oldest son, Menachem. (Menachem, living in Petah Tikva, was already married and had a one-year-old child.)

Yona brought the handsomely printed invitation to the authorities. They agreed to allow Yona, Tourou, and their daughter Judith to go. They would, of course, have to find three guarantors and guarantee they would return to Addis in three months.

"I will be your guarantor," Yona's friend Abebe offered. The two men stood near the fence in Yona's courtyard, talking in low voices.

"You are a good man, Abebe," Yona said, "and a dear friend. But I can't let you take the risk. What if I don't come back?"

"I am a Christian. They won't harm me." Abebe leaned against the fence.

Yona shook his head. "You have to think not only of yourself. You have to think about your wife and your children. Three small children! Who will take care of them if the police arrest you on my account?"

"Don't you think that I worry about my wife and children? I love them more than anything in the world. But Yona, things will get better here, and after a while, you'll come back."

"I can't allow you to put your life in danger."

"I've heard of Jewish guarantors disappearing. But have you ever heard of Christian guarantors put into jail?"

"I haven't. That doesn't mean it hasn't happened. I appreciate your offer, Abebe. But I can't accept it."

"If a friend can't help you, who can? You must let me do this."

Tears stained Yona's face. "I feel very heavy in my heart."

"But you agree?" Abebe smiled.

Reluctantly, he said, "I agree."

Yona walked up the wooden steps to his house and settled himself in his favorite chair. His eyes grew wet with memories. He had been a pupil in the Holy Land in 1922 when it was called Palestine. He had danced in the streets of Jerusalem with other children, singing, celebrating the miracle. The world had given the British a mandate to establish a "Jewish National Home in Palestine."

Now, fifty-seven years later, he had found a Christian friend willing to risk his own life so that Yona could return.

Two other friends became the guarantors for Tourou and their daughter Judith. They applied for three passports and began the long days and nights of waiting.

BOOK TWO
The Way It Began

Chapter Six

Yona's passage to Israel had begun when he was twelve.

Like all the boys in the little Jewish village of Weleka, he had worked as a shepherd, bringing the family's sheep and oxen to pasture, farming as Jews had farmed in biblical days.

Born in 1908, he was one of twelve children, and bone-poor. During the rainy season, his father worked as a sharecropper on the patch of land owned by a Christian landlord. During the dry season, his mother spun and his father wove the cotton to clothe their burgeoning family. They lived on the edge of hunger, their lives defined and partitioned by the tropical rains and the African drought.

At the start of the rains, Yona and his brothers harnessed the oxen to the plow they had made from a piece of eucalyptus wood, prepared the ground, and then seeded it with barley and wheat and *teff*. When the rains ended, they harnessed the oxen again and harvested the crop.

There was no school in Weleka. Only the *Kes*, the Jewish priest, and a few men could read Ge'ez, the ancient religious and literary language of Ethiopia. Most parents and children were illiterate. Yona too was illiterate.

Then in 1920, a visitor came to Weleka. He was Professor Jacques Faitlovitch, a French scholar, who was to change Yona's life and the lives of the Ethiopian Jews forever.

YONA HAD NEVER heard of Faitlovitch nor had he heard of Faitlovitch's teacher, Professor Joseph Halévy, who had visited Ethiopia in the 1860s.

The Falashas were once again being "discovered" by overzealous missionaries from Europe who were scouting Africa to win Jews and pagans to Christianity. Most of the missionaries were Anglicans, who, on their return to their homes, published triumphant reports of how they were converting exotic black Jews.

The stories alarmed the Jewish establishment in France and England. Professor Halévy, a French-Jewish linguist and poet fluent in Ethiopian languages, decided to travel to Abyssinia, as Ethiopia was then called, to investigate.

"Here I am," he appealed through the press. "Send me."

He was selected, his journey sponsored and financed by the Alliance Israélite Universelle.

The Alliance was an early Jewish self-help agency, a forerunner of today's antidiscrimination leagues. Its aim was to emancipate Jews in lands where they were slaves, and open a network of schools in countries where illiteracy was the norm. On both counts, slavery and illiteracy, Abyssinia was a natural for the Alliance.

It was 1868 when Halévy reached Massawa, the coastal port on the Red Sea. Travel was dangerous. So Halévy, with a patrician face and flowing white mustache, passed himself off as a rhinoceros dealer. He traveled on a camel.

As soon as he reached the first Jewish village, he dropped his disguise.

"I am a Jew," he told the people.

"What! You are a Falasha! A *white* Falasha! You are laughing at us! Are there any white Falashas?"

He finally convinced the villagers that he too was a circumcised Jew.

"I assured them"—he described that first encounter in his book *Travels in Abyssinia*—"that all the Falashas of Jerusalem . . . were white. . . . The name of Jerusalem, which I had accidentally mentioned, changed as if by magic the attitude of the most incredulous."

"Oh, do you come from Jerusalem, the Blessed City?" they queried him. "Have you beheld with your own eyes Mount Zion, and the House of the Lord of Israel, the Holy Temple?"

"I must confess," he wrote, "I was deeply moved on seeing those black faces light up at the memory of our glorious history."

Halévy told them that there were indeed Jews living in the Holy Land. But then he told them something even more incredible. There were Jews living in other countries as well.

"And all white! Impossible!"

The incredulity of the black Jews was a mirror image of the incredulity of academicians and rabbis in Europe. How could these black Ethiopians really be Jews? Maybe they were converts; maybe they were members of a black sect.

Halévy came away in the spring in 1868 convinced that the skeptics in France were wrong.

He estimated that there were between 150,000 and 200,000 Ethiopian Jews, and found them more rigid in obeying the laws of the Books of Moses than most traditionally Orthodox Jews in Europe or America.

As proof of their Jewishness, he brought back from Ethiopia

a Jewish prayer book in the ancient language of Ge'ez and a young Ethiopian Jew who was to be educated in Europe. The youngster, unable to withstand European weather, and perhaps European hostility, died soon after.

Halévy succeeded in convincing some of the skeptics, and he might have convinced more had not the Franco-Prussian war intervened. The Jewish leaders in the Alliance had more pressing problems than the fate of the black Jews.

As time passed, Halévy's credibility began to be questioned. Rumors were circulated that he had never been in Ethiopia, and that the young Ethiopian was a black slave he had bought in the slave market in Sudan.

Halévy was forced to turn to the French consul in Massawa to confirm that he had really been in Abyssinia.

Deeply hurt, he found little or no interest in the Jews of Ethiopia until, at the turn of the century, nearly forty years later, he inspired Jacques Faitlovitch, one of his brilliant young students, to take up the fight.

Faitlovitch, a young man of twenty-three, scholarly and adventurous, was a perfect candidate for Halévy. He had worked out his adolescent rebellion against his rabbinic family in Lodz, Poland, by secretly leaving home and traveling to Paris intending to become a rabbi and a doctor.

Instead, studying at the École des Hautes Études, he had become a social anthropologist, so enthralled by the black Jews that he decided to go to Ethiopia. He prepared himself by mastering Amharic and Tigrinya, the languages of Gondar and Tigray, where most of the Jews lived. He read everything he could find until he was ready to travel.

In 1903, he went to Baron Édmond de Rothschild and convinced the foremost Jew in Paris to finance his trip. Dressed like a tropical explorer in leather boots, riding pants, a cotton jacket buttoned to his neck, and a pith helmet, the adventurous young scholar journeyed by land and sea until he set foot in Massawa on the Red Sea coast in January 1904.

From Massawa, he made his way on mule and horseback to

the Jewish villages in Tigray and those that lay in Gondar north of Lake Tana and the Blue Nile.

At the start, it was no easier for him than it had been for Halévy. Some of the villagers had seen a few white men, but those white men were all missionaries. "Every time a European comes to see us," they told him, "he proclaims himself a Jew; but that is only to deceive us or convert us."

Faitlovitch had to break new ground. How could he win the confidence of the people, dispel the suspicions of all strangers, convince them he had come, not as a greedy colonial lord or a missionary, but genuinely to help?

First, he spoke their language. The people were startled and then delighted that Faitlovitch could talk to them freely and intimately, without interpreters.

Then, instead of denigrating their customs and their unique forms of Jewish worship, he proved, through his sympathetic questions and careful observations, that he had come to study and learn.

He had a third advantage. Despite his unorthodox departure from his rabbinic family in Poland, he had remained an observant Orthodox Jew. The Sabbath was as holy to him as it was to the villagers. He observed it in his own way and they in theirs. The Jew from Paris sat on the mud ledge of the straw tukul that was the synagogue, solemnly reciting the Sabbath prayers with the black Jews of Ethiopia.

Thus he won them over, and was in turn won over by them.

How could he help them?

Education was the answer he chose. Only through education could they break out of the cycle of poverty and ignorance and keep their faith.

He decided to educate young Ethiopian Jews in Europe and return them to Ethiopia to educate others.

He wanted to bring the whole community into modern religious orthodoxy, teach them Hebrew and modern behavior so they could enter the newborn twentieth century.

He estimated there were now about ninety thousand Jews

in Ethiopia, their numbers depleted since Halévy's visit by famine, disease, and conversion.

After a year and a half in Ethiopia, Faitlovitch returned to Paris. He brought out with him two teenagers, Getye Yeremias, who lived in a village near Gondar, and Tamrat Emmanuel, whose parents had converted to Christianity. Faitlovitch found Tamrat, a short, slender youngster with a dramatic flair, in the Swedish mission in Asmara; his mother had become an Abyssinian nun. In Paris, Faitlovitch placed both boys under the tutelage of the Alliance.

For the leaders of the Jewish establishment, he brought a message in Amharic signed by several of the Jewish high priests and a scribe named Debtera Teka.

> May the Lord God of Israel be praised. . . . Peace! Peace! . . . How are you? We are in a state of profound misery . . . attempts were made forcibly to convert us. We gave our hearts, and the God of Abraham, Isaac, and Jacob has saved us. Thanks to your prayers, a small number of us still remain. . . . Our books have been destroyed. . . . Oh! our brethren do not forget us.

Faitlovitch reported his findings to Baron de Rothschild in 1905, and then published the report in his *Notes d'un voyage chez les Falashas*. He described the people in their straw-thatched tukuls, illiterate, desperately poor, isolated in their mountain fastnesses. Defying the indefatigable missionaries, they had maintained a passion for their faith and a yearning for the land of their fathers.

"These brothers must be retained in the religion of Israel," he insisted, as he began to race around Europe and later America, setting up "pro-Falasha committees" to make the world aware of the existence of his beloved black Jews and their plight.

Three years later, he was back in Ethiopia for a momentous experience.

The elders in the Jewish villages asked him to see Menelik II, the emperor of Abyssinia.

IN 1908, he journeyed down the mountains to Addis Ababa and petitioned the palace for an audience with the monarch. After ten days, it was granted.

The palace was a huge stone building, encircled by a high wall and surrounded by a jumble of smaller buildings. Entering through two heavily guarded doors, Faitlovitch was ushered into the presence of the emperor and his courtiers.

Menelik had already won his stripes as a warrior king in a land where for some two thousand years kings and tribal rulers had been weaving wily intrigues against one another, massacring each other in murderous wars.

Menelik had tried to bring Ethiopia out of the dark ages. In 1893, at the urging of his Empress Taitu, he moved the capital from Gondar to Addis Ababa—the name meant "New Flower." He began building a railroad from Djibouti on the Red Sea, and opened a telegraph system. In 1896, he astonished the European colonial powers who were carving up black Africa by stopping the Italians dead in their tracks.

The Italians already possessed Eritrea and had turned the province into an Italian colony. Now they wanted more land. From Eritrea, fifteen thousand Italian troops in full battle dress, with fifty-six cannon, marched into the highlands of Ethiopia.

Menelik sent a hundred thousand black troops to drive them back. In the flowing tribal robes of Ethiopia, his warriors dashed across the hills on spirited horses. Others carried forty-two cannon and a cache of rifles that Menelik had bought from the Italians in earlier years of friendship.

Across the untamed landscape of eastern Ethiopia, the armies faced each other with primitive spears and modern deafening cannonfire until Menelik defeated the Italians in the battle of Adowa, a hundred miles south of Asmara.

Eight thousand Italians and four thousand native Eritrean troops were slaughtered. The "shame of Adowa" was to rankle in Italian hearts for years.

This was the man Faitlovitch was now addressing, a royal figure on a red and gold throne, with dark, shrewd eyes and deep lines that dug into his skin from his nose past his mustache to his straggly beard.

Faitlovitch presented his carefully prepared case. Speaking in Amharic, an unusual feat for a European, which must have impressed Menelik and his courtiers, Failovitch described how Jews were being persecuted and killed. He himself had been in a village where a local chieftain had come with his band of armed tribesmen to seize the uncle of his gifted pupil, Tamrat Emmanuel. A Christian woman had dreamt that Tamrat's uncle had turned into a hyena, had drunk her child's blood, and killed it. It was sheer luck that Faitlovitch was there to persuade the chief that it was only a dream.

Building his speech to a crescendo, he described how Jewish ironsmiths and masons were torn from their families and their villages, forced to live as slaves in Addis and other areas far from home, compelled to desecrate the Sabbath, while they erected palaces and villas for the rich and powerful.

Once they were slaves in Egypt. Now they were slaves in Ethiopia.

Faitlovitch's speech found its resonance in the royal court. Menelik issued a royal edict proclaiming the end of slavery.

For several years, his proclamation was obeyed. But slavery was endemic in Africa, and soon, once again, Jews were being captured and sold as slaves.

Still, Faitlovitch had achieved what no other European or Jew before him had accomplished. He had presented the Jewish case before the emperor. And he had established a link in America and Europe with the long-suffering Jews of Ethiopia.

From now on, for most of the Ethiopian Jews, he could do

no wrong. He was their father, their prophet, their redeemer.

PARIS TO Ethiopia. Ethiopia to Paris. Faitlovitch rarely stopped.

In 1914, he opened the first Jewish village school, appointing Getye Yeremias, one of the young men he had taken to Europe, as its teacher.

In 1914, the First World War made travel to Ethiopia impossible. Faitlovitch spent the war years in Geneva teaching Amharic and Tigrinya at the university. In 1920, he returned to Ethiopia, this time with three companions—a physician to heal the sick, his brother, and his protégé, Tamrat Emmanuel, who had now finished his schooling in Europe.

The rainy season caught him in Yona's village, Weleka. Travel was impossible. So, unwilling to waste time, he opened a Jewish school for boys. Even a compassionate scholar like Faitlovitch obviously did not think girls needed to read or write. It was enough for girls to marry and bear a child every year. Boys were different. Boys could become leaders. Boys could teach other boys to read and write and rise up from ignorance and poverty and secure Jewish survival.

The school was, of necessity, a night school.

During the day, the boys worked in the fields or assisted their fathers, many of whom were blacksmiths, honing and firing metal into knives and spears that Christian and Moslem and pagan warriors would use, and into plows for all the farmers, Jews as well.

When the sun set, the boys met by lantern and candlelight in a small tukul where Faitlovitch taught them Hebrew and Hebrew songs, and captivated them with stories of the Holy Book and the Holy Land.

"The joy of the Falashas to see me again in their midst was indescribable," Faitlovitch wrote in an American pro-Falasha committee publication. "From all points delegates of various

Jewish communities came to greet me, to confer with me, and to report the needs of their people. In the fall, a large group of Falasha notables gathered in the village where I had my quarters to pass the High Holy Days with me . . . the Days of Awe."

Even as Yom Kippur, the Day of Atonement, ended, Faitlovitch called his young pupils together. "Soon I shall leave. I shall go to Addis Ababa and back to Europe. I would like to take four of you with me."

One of the four he selected was Yona.

Chapter Seven

YONA, NOT YET thirteen, but already taller than most lads his age, sat on the earthen floor in his father's tukul. He listened as his teacher talked to his father.

"I am not taking your son away from you forever," he heard Faitlovitch say. "He will come back, I promise you. He has a gift for languages. Let me take him to Jerusalem, then to Europe. Let him get a real education, something he can never get here. Then he will return, a teacher and a leader, and teach others to become teachers and leaders."

Yona's father shook his head. "But I need him."

An older relative raised his voice.

"That's not the reason. You have enough other sons to help

you. I know your reason; you're afraid he won't come back, and you'll lose him."

Yona moved toward his father. "I will come back, Father. I promise you."

"No. No. I can't let you leave me."

"Why?" the relative exploded. "How can you, as a father, stop him from traveling with a man like Professor Faitlovitch? How many boys get such an opportunity? It will change his whole life."

Yona sucked in his breath, waiting.

"I must know you will come back." The words seemed to wrench themselves from his father's lips.

Yona hugged his father. "I will come back. Nothing will stop me."

Faitlovitch left the tukul, prophesying, "He will make you proud."

YONA'S YEARS IN the great world outside of Weleka telescoped themselves into hard study. First Jerusalem. Two and a half years in the Takhimonie School, an Orthodox yeshiva. Then Europe. Two years in a private religious school in Frankfurt, Germany; two more years in Baix-les-Bains, Switzerland, in a Jewish boarding school run by a Dr. Ascher; and finally two years in Paris. Yona could now speak not only Amharic, but six other languages—Hebrew, German, Yiddish, French, Italian, and English.

In 1932, he returned to Ethiopia, a worldy young man of twenty-four, ready to fulfill the promise Faitlovitch had given his father. He would become a teacher and a leader.

In Addis, he became a teacher in the Jewish boarding school and teachers' training school Faitlovitch had opened in 1920. Its director was Professor Tamrat Emmanuel, the intellectually gifted student Faitlovitch had taken to Paris in 1905. Yona became assistant director and teacher—teaching Hebrew, French, and religious law.

The boarding school was famous. Children, teenagers, even grown men walked hundreds of kilometers to enter. Older students, after two years of teacher training, were sent to the villages to open elementary schools.

While more than 95 percent of Ethiopia was still illiterate, Jewish children in the most remote villages in the mountains could now read and write.

THEN CAME 1936.

Benito Mussolini, dreaming of becoming a modern Caesar, and jealous that England, France, and Belgium had rich colonies in Africa, decided to acquire more colonies of his own. Unfortunately for Mussolini's dreams, he was late. Africa was nearly all parceled out.

The only independent kingdom left was Ethiopia.

Logistically and geopolitically, Ethiopia lay close to the land Italy had grabbed off earlier—Eritrea and Italian Somaliland. Now, with visions of a new Roman Empire, Mussolini decided he would conquer Ethiopia and once and for all avenge the 1896 "shame of Adowa," the Italian defeat by Emperor Menelik's warriors.

In impassioned speeches from his balcony in Rome, Mussolini explained to his cheering followers why they needed Ethiopia. Italy was a poor and overpopulated country; it needed colonies for emigration. Ethiopia was a poor, backward country where slavery still existed. It needed the Italians to modernize and liberate it.

He called up reservists, swelling his army to 1 million men, and shipped them through the Suez Canal into Eritrea. On January 12, 1936, his chief of the general staff, Marshal Pietro Badoglio, bulldozed his troops across Ethiopia with tanks, trucks, and planes such as Ethiopians had never seen. Poison gas had been outlawed by the League of Nations. Poison gas was used.

Dropping a bomb as he flew low, Count Galeazzo Ciano,

Mussolini's son-in-law, exulted at the fiery destruction. It looked to him, he exclaimed euphorically, like a beautiful rose unfolding.

To fight Mussolini's tanks and planes, Haile Selassie issued mobilization orders:

> "Everyone will now be mobilized and all boys old enough to carry a spear will be sent to Addis Ababa. Married men will take their wives to carry food and cook. Those without wives will take any woman without a husband. Women with small babies need not go. The blind, those who cannot walk, or for any reason cannot carry a spear are exempted. Anyone found at home after the receipt of this order will be hanged."

On May 2, the Negus, Emperor Haile Selassie, Lion of the Tribe of Judah, the Elect of God, King of the Kings of Ethiopia, fled with his family by train to neighboring Djibouti, angering many of his followers who continued to resist the Italians.

On May 5, the Italian army entered Addis Ababa and raised the tricolor. And on June 28, the defeated emperor addressed the League of Nations in Geneva. "I was defending the cause of all small peoples who are threatened by aggression."

Bitterly, he predicted, "God and History will remember your judgment."

The League passed a few halfhearted and impotent sanctions, but the attention of the world was riveted on Hitler's 1936 march on the Rhineland.

The emperor first took refuge in Jerusalem, the city of David and Solomon. Was he not a direct descendant of King Solomon?

The citizens of Jerusalem knew little of the emperor and almost nothing of the centuries-old persecution and slavery of the black Jews. Most had never even heard the word "Falasha."

Nor did they learn the irony that Haile Selassie, whose pre-coronation name was Ras Tafari Mekonnen, had become the god of a new religion called by a combination of his princely title, Ras, and Tafari, his first name, "Rastafarianism."

Bowing politely each day, Jerusalemites greeted the little emperor and the empress as they took their regal walk down the streets of the Holy City followed by their children and their little dogs, until the entourage moved on to London.

In Italy, schoolchildren and soldiers sang a different song about the black Ethiopians and their emperor:

> *Little black face*
> *You will be Italian.*
> *Vestal fire,*
> *The Negus is a beast.*
> *When he walks*
> *He looks to me like a chicken.*

And from his balcony, overlooking the Piazza Venezia in Rome, Mussolini proclaimed: "At last Italy has her Empire."

YONA, NOW twenty-eight years old, was caught in the wave of fascist terrorism.

Marshal Rodolfo Graziani, the Italian chief of staff, opened concentration camps in Ethiopia and murdered thousands of innocent people. A special target were those who had been educated abroad, Christians, Moslems, and Jews.

In Addis, Graziani closed Faitlovitch's Jewish boarding school. Several Jewish teachers and students were killed. Tamrat was placed on the most-wanted list. Yona was still safe.

Tamrat bade farewell to Yona and his beloved students, and fled the country through Djibouti to Palestine. In Tel Aviv, he joined Faitlovitch, who had married and was living in a comfortable white house on Witkin Street close to the Mediterranean Sea.

Later Tamrat would go to Cairo. Haile Selassie, knowing

his gifts as an educator and organizer, invited him to become part of the Ethiopian government-in-exile.

Meanwhile Yona had to forage for food for his destitute students. He took any job he could find. The tall, scholarly gentleman found himself hawking Ethiopian coffee.

Then the Italians intercepted a letter he wrote to Professor Tamrat Emmanuel. He too was placed on the Italians' most-wanted list.

He began to run, fleeing from one province to another, until he was given safe haven by Moslems in the gold-mining region of Welega, west of Addis. His ear for languages stood him in good stead. He soon learned to speak their Hamitic tongue, and spent three years among them, supervising some two hundred goldminers.

But the war in Ethiopia was not going well for Mussolini. The Italian conquerors discovered they were no match against native partisans.

Guerrillas would suddenly appear, take shots at the Italian soldiers, and disappear in the mountains they knew well. Executions and concentration camps were no deterrent.

By November 1937, Mussolini recognized that the policy of repression was a failure.

Graziani was replaced. The concentration camps were closed, and thousands of Italian peasants were brought in rotating shifts into the country. They settled the land, built roads and villas and government buildings, and left the mark of their hand forever on Ethiopia.

In 1941, Mussolini finally entered the war on the side of Germany.

Now, at last, the allies could come to Ethiopia's defense.

Britain, with vital interests in Africa, took on the battle. One of the top commanders was Colonel Orde Wingate, the brilliant maverick soldier whose twin passions were the Bible and the land of Israel.

In Palestine, during the Arab riots in 1936, Wingate had trained young Haganah soldiers like Moshe Dayan and Yigal

Allon to fight Arab terrorists in "Special Night Squads."
At Wingate's request, some of his Jewish Night Squad com-
mandos were rushed to Ethiopia to help free another biblical land. In a three-pronged attack, the British routed the
Italians.

The war for Ethiopia was over. In 1942, the Lion of Judah,
with Wingate and Tamrat Emmanuel beside him, made his
triumphant entrance into Addis Ababa.

Back in control, but with a dearth of talented men in his
government, the emperor recruited many of the educated young
Jews Faitlovitch had trained. He invited Tamrat to reorga-
nize his foreign service and to become deputy minister of education; he persuaded Faitlovitch himself to serve as advisor
to his embassy in Cairo; and he made Yona director of the
Translation Department in the Ministry of Education.

In 1942, Yona married the beautiful Tourou and began raising a family.

While war and murder raged in Europe and the Far East,
Ethiopia was at last at peace.

ON MAY 14, 1948, Yona sat at the radio listening. The voice
of David Ben-Gurion filled the living room in Addis.

*"The land of Israel was the birthplace of the Jewish people.
. . . Here they wrote and gave the Bible to the world."*

Yona's chest heaved. "Tourou," he called. "Tourou, come
quickly."

She hurried out of the kitchen. "What is it?"

"Listen," he breathed.

*"The State of Israel will be open to Jewish immigration and
for the ingathering of the exiles."*

Her eyes filled with tears. "Does it mean—?" she asked

"Yes. Yes. It means Jews will be going home again. After
two thousand years."

The shepherd boy from Weleka had lived to see Israel re-
born.

Chapter Eight

EACH EVENING, Yona and Tourou sat, first in anguish and then in elation, as they followed the war in Israel on the radio. The armies of seven Arab states had invaded, completely encircling the newborn country. Yet, by the summer of 1948, scarcely three months after the birth of the nation, the Israelis were pushing the invaders back. And even as they fought, they set up the machinery of government.

It was fitting, Yona reasoned, that the first law passed in the Knesset was "the Law of Return."

The Law of Return.

Every Jew from any country in the world was now free to come to Israel to live. As soon as he stepped onto the soil, he would be a citizen.

106

"What do you think?" Tourou asked hesitantly. "Does it mean the Jews of Ethiopia too?"

"It must," Yona said. "Ben-Gurion talked about the ingathering of the exiles. We too are exiles. But first they have to win the war."

By the fall of 1948, most of the Arab armies were driven out of the land. On January 12, 1949, Ralph Bunche, the American grandson of African slaves, assembled the former combatants in the Hotel des Roses on the island of Rhodes. Bunche, whose title was United Nations Chief Representative of the Secretary General in Palestine, sequestered each Arab representative into a room alone with an Israeli. He knew that if the Arabs sat together, they would lose face, and never agree to an armistice. His diplomacy succeeded. Presiding in his hotel suite, he allowed himself a slight victory smile as each of the defeated Arab delegations signed armistice accords with Israel. Egypt, which had begun the war, was the first to sign; the rest followed—Lebanon, Jordan, Syria. Only one nation refused; this was Iraq.

In the next months, Yona learned how great rivers of Jews were pouring home into the sea that was Israel. Where else in the world, he marveled, has there been a tiny nation, just born, still fighting for its life, taking in a flood tide of refugees?

From Europe came the battered and scarred survivors of the Holocaust. Sometimes 1,000 a day came into Haifa until some 200,000 had come from the displaced-persons camps of Germany, from the British prison camps of Cyprus, from the forests and caves of Stalin's Russia. Men who had never held a gun were given a weapon and some kind of uniform. Many who had survived Hitler and Stalin died so that Israel could live.

Still more came from Arab lands—from Morocco, Tunisia, Libya, Algeria; 50,000 came from Yemen and 120,000 from Iraq, fulfilling the biblical prophecy that they would "rise up on eagles' wings." American Skymasters became those wings of eagles.

Wars create refugees. In a mirror image of the 600,000 Arab

refugees who fled from Israel, 600,000 Jewish refugees fled from Arab lands into Israel. In four years, the little country trebled its population from 400,000 to 1,200,000.

But when, Yona pondered, would it take in the Jews of Ethiopia?

ISRAEL'S SCHOLARLY president, Itzhak Ben-Zvi, took the first step in 1953. He asked the Jewish Agency's Department for Torah Education in the Diaspora to open schools for the Jewish children in Ethiopia.

In earlier years, the Jewish Agency had been the shadow Jewish government under the British. Now the Jewish Agency, in charge of absorbing immigrants, sent an emissary, Rabbi Shmuel Be'eri, to meet with Yona in Addis.

"We plan to open a boarding school and a teacher-training institute in Asmara on the Red Sea," Rabbi Be'eri told Yona. "We want you to become its director."

"You honor me," Yona replied.

But he was torn. The school would give him the chance to fulfill his dream—educating young Jews, preparing them for life in Israel. On the other hand, could he leave his prestigious position as one of the directors in the Ministry of Education?

"Emperor Haile Selassie," he told the emissary, "looks with disfavor on anyone who leaves his government."

"The Jews need you more than the emperor does."

"You don't know Haile Selassie. He can be a friend, if he trusts you. But if you cross him, he can be a dangerous enemy."

"And you're not prepared to live with that?"

Yona stared out the window into his courtyard. The brittle cacophonic noises of Addis Ababa, of people hawking vegetables, of horses and donkeys clomping on the road, filled the living room.

"The question is," he said thoughtfully, "which is better for the Jews? My working, as a Jew, inside the establishment?

Or my working as the director of a Jewish school?"

"You know the answer yourself. Faitlovitch prepared you for just this kind of leadership. You owe it to the Jewish children of Ethiopia."

Yona leaned back in his armchair. The afternoon sun, filtering through the lace curtains, made his skin look like burnished gold.

"I will write the emperor. I will petition him to allow me to leave his service."

Haile Selassie did not deign to answer. Yona appealed to the minister of education, who approved his leaving and was himself instantly demoted and dispatched to another province. Yona became *persona non grata* in the government in Addis. As word of his "betrayal" spread through the country, even Gondar closed its doors to him.

But in the coastal town of Asmara, where he had moved with Tourou and their growing family, he was the director of the new teacher-training school. Girls this time, as well as boys, were among the fifty-seven young people studying to become teachers. Several of the students were *kessoch*, Jewish priests who walked for hundreds of miles to study Hebrew with Yona and modern rabbinic Judaism with Rabbi Be'eri.

Two years later, in 1955, the Jewish Agency decided to do more. They would speed up the process of education. They would bring young people to Israel, train them, and send them back to Ethiopia to reach more and more Jewish children.

Yona selected twenty-seven boys and girls, ten to seventeen years old, and sent them in two separate groups to Israel. Among the first group were fourteen-year-old Emanuel, who later would shepherd Alitash and Daniel to the safe houses in Sudan, and thirteen-year-old Joseph who, in 1979, would be tortured and crippled in Gondar.

Yona explained to the young people, some of whom were going outside their little villages for the first time in their lives: "You are the first groups invited officially to Israel. You're going to live in an Orthodox village north of Tel Aviv.

It's called Kfar Batya and it's run by the Mizrachi Women's Organization of America. You bear a special responsibility. You are our ambassadors. Through you, Israel will learn about Ethiopian Jews. And you will learn about Israel. You are paving the way for others to come."

Yona hugged and kissed them, and bade them farewell.

NINE OF THE young people came back to Ethiopia in 1958. Emanuel reported immediately to Yona. They embraced and kissed each other like father and son. "Let me look at you." Yona studied the seventeen-year-old's lithe body, the young princely face. "I see you grew in Israel in many ways. Sit down. Do sit down." Yona offered him a chair. "Start from the beginning."

"It was everything you said it would be." Emanuel spoke animatedly. "We lived with three hundred other students. They were from all over the world. Many were orphans from the big war in Europe, Youth Aliyah children."

Yona nodded sadly. Youth Aliyah had begun in Germany in 1933 as a children's migration, the rescue of children whose parents were doomed by Hitler to deportation and death. Henrietta Szold, the founder of Hadassah, traveled to Germany when in her seventies, bent on saving lives. "If we can't save the parents," she cried, "at least let us try to save the children."

After the war, Youth Aliyah continued bringing in and absorbing over one hundred thousand youngsters in the greatest youth migration movement in history.

"All of us in Kfar Batya studied hard." Emanuel's words were tumbling over one another. "Hebrew, English, mathematics, Talmud, history, geography. And we worked hard. We plowed the fields. We learned different kinds of agriculture. We learned carpentry, mechanics, weaving, electricity. I wanted to swallow it all."

Yona's eyes crinkled with pleasure at his disciple's enthusiasm.

"Now my dream," Emanuel said, "is to prepare the children here for life in Israel. I want to take them there myself."

Yona embraced him. "I pray you will be able to do it."

He could see Emanuel leading hundreds of children like figures on a Renaissance painting, walking, dancing, their arms reaching out toward their own El Dorado.

"And Yona, the greatest experience was meeting Professor Faitlovitch."

"God gave you that gift—to meet him yourself!"

"He came to visit us in school. He even recognized some of us. After he left, we studied harder than ever. He made us feel so good, so important." Emanuel was speaking even more rapidly now. "And we had many other visitors. President Ben-Zvi came with his wife and they asked all kinds of questions. The president writes books about Jewish communities in distant places like China."

"I never thought," Yona said, "that you would meet the president of Israel."

"Not only the president. One day Mrs. Eleanor Roosevelt came from America, and our own Yael gave her a bouquet of lilies. Mrs. Roosevelt told us how happy she was to meet young people from Ethiopia. After that, some journalists from America came and wrote articles about us. And then Professor Faitlovich invited some of us to his house . . ."

Yona waited as Emanuel began to speak more slowly. "He looked so tired, so old and bent over. All around him were walls and walls of books in tall bookcases. He sat behind a dark wooden desk. But his eyesight was nearly gone. He had to strain to even see us. 'You are my children and my grandchildren,' he said to us—his voice was so weak. And then"—Emanuel's throat grew tight—"two days later, he died."

Tears fell into Yona's black beard. He brushed them away.

THE NEW MINISTER of education, Mekonnen Endelkachow, a Christian, sent word to Yona. "The emperor wishes to see the students who have returned from studying in Israel."

Every student allowed to go abroad was expected to appear before the emperor to receive his blessings and his exhortations to return. The first group to go to Kfar Batya had left Ethiopia from Asmara on the Red Sea. It would have been too costly for them to go back across Ethiopia to see the emperor in Addis. Yona had promised the minister of education they would pay their respects when they returned.

Now, summoned to appear, Emanuel, Joseph who would later be tortured, six other boys, and Yael traveled by bus from the mountains of Gondar to Addis, stayed in a cheap hotel to save money, and waited two months for their audience with the Lion of Judah.

At last the great day arrived. Shepherded by Yona, the nine young people entered the palace. They walked through a courtyard where courtiers, princes, noblemen, landowners scrutinized them closely. Who were these eight young men, dressed in open-collared white cotton shirts with rolled-up sleeves, dark pants, and skullcaps on their heads? And who was this young woman in a white shirt and blue skirt, with white socks and shoes? Who were they who could appear in such untraditional clothing before His Imperial Majesty.

The minister of education led them through the courtyard, past police, lackeys, gardeners, and soldiers of the Imperial Guard armed with rifles and swords, then through the palace into the throne room. Yona, still *persona non grata*, remained in the corridor.

In awe, the young people entered a hall that seemed to Emanuel larger than three fields of barley. They saw the emperor sitting on a high gold and scarlet throne in a cream-colored uniform with thirteen tiers of battle ribbons across his chest, just as in the posters that hung all over the land.

He was smaller than they had imagined, and now, approaching him, they saw that his skin was mocha, his lips and chin almost concealed by kinky black hair, his eyes deep and penetrating beneath a thicket of black brows. His face was grooved with lines that crossed his broad forehead, dug into the bridge of his nose, and slashed his cheeks. He was the King of Kings, His Venerable Majesty, His Revered Highness, the Lion of Judah, sole ruler of the land, arbiter of life and death.

Next to him stood his ebony-faced minister of the pen, ready to write down his commands. Other ministers and functionaries stood at rigid attention, and towering over the emperor was the imperial bodyguard, a monstrous giantlike figure with a massive mustache.

At the emperor's feet was his small dog, and on his desk were two gold lions. A live lion sat in the corner of the huge throne room.

The young people walked single file toward the emperor while the imperial bodyguard kept shouting at them, "Speak! Speak!"

They realized they were expected to kneel before His Venerable Majesty with their faces to the ground. But their years in Israel had taught them that Jews bowed only before God. They nodded their heads politely and in silence. The emperor seemed unperturbed, his ink-black eyes peering down at them in their Israeli clothes.

At the request of the minister of education, they had translated their diplomas into English and brought them along. Now, as Mekonnen Endelkachow introduced them, one by one, to Haile Selassie, the minister read the diploma descriptions of what they had studied in Israel. He stressed how many different kinds of agriculture they had mastered.

Emanuel watched the emperor closely. He had heard that the emperor read nothing, wrote nothing, and never signed papers in his own handwriting.

Haile Selassie had received some private lessons as a child from a French Jesuit priest, but no further schooling. Everything was read to him or spoken. It was his technique of ruling, and it served him well. He could change orders with a flip of his wrist. There were no written records of his commands, except those jotted down by the minister of the pen, and even those he could easily deny.

The diploma-reading ended. The emperor spoke in a voice

so low the young people strained to hear him: "My children, it is good that you have studied in Israel, which is like a brother to us. You have come back to our country with important education and knowledge."

The minister of the pen nodded seriously. The imperial bodyguard called out, "Speak! Speak!" But the young people said nothing. They were unsure what they were expected to say.

"I have something to offer you," the emperor said, scarcely moving his lips. He turned to his minister of education. "Mekonnen, I want you to give each of these students a job."

The nine young people looked at each other in bewilderment. They had been summoned to pay their respects to His Imperial Majesty. Instead, he was offering them jobs.

The emperor went on. "You can teach our farmers and peasants how to farm their land. Some of you can work in the police and in the government. We have jobs for all of you."

"Speak! Speak!" the bodyguard shouted.

But the young people were silent.

The emperor looked down at them. "I will be happy to give you everything you need—good salaries, good houses, good cars. It is important for our country that you have brought back so much knowledge. Now I will hear from you."

"Speak! Speak!" said the imperial bodyguard.

Thoughts swirled through Emanuel's head. All the years in Israel, learning Hebrew, studying Jewish history and culture and religion, coming back aflame with Zionism—were they expected to give it all up now?

It was Emanuel who answered. "Your Highness, we thank you for your most kind and generous offer."

The emperor smiled.

Emanuel's voice, tentative at first, grew stronger. "Your Majesty, we deeply appreciate what you are offering us. However, we were sent to Israel for one purpose—to come back to teach our people."

Emanuel knew it was a reckless answer, but an honest one.

LEFT: *Joseph Halévy, the first white Jew to visit Ethiopia in the 1860s. Until his arrival, the Ethiopian Jews did not know there were any white Jews in the world.* BELOW: *Jacques Faitlovitch, Halévy's disciple, on horseback in Ethiopia, 1903. Faitlovitch won the confidence of the Ethiopian Jews, and devoted the rest of his life to saving them from extinction.*

ABOVE: *Yona ben Naftali in 1954 in the school he built in Asmara on the Red Sea. It was from here that the first groups of youngsters left for Israel to study at Kfar Batya in 1955.* OPPOSITE, ABOVE: *The boarding school in Addis Ababa which Faitlovitch established in 1921. At left is the director, Tamrat Emman-uel, who later became Emperor Haile Selassie's Deputy Minister of Education.* OPPOSITE, BELOW: *The women of Weleka inviting American visitors to buy their clay figurines. The names of the villagers cannot be revealed, since doing so might endanger them.*

ABOVE: *The anguish of separation. Parents who were unable to make the long, hazardous trek hold the photos of their children who are somewhere in Israel.* RIGHT: *A village woman admiring the pearls an American visitor has given her. Word of the arrival of tourists spreads through the villages faster than the beating of a drum.*

TOP: *The marketplace in Gondar City. Peasants walk for hours to bring their vegetables, spices, and wares to the market in the heart* of the city. ABOVE: *The clothing area where Daniel bought the gossamer white shamma for Alitash before their journey.*

Those left in the villages after Operation Moses are mostly children and elderly women.

TOP: *Soviet helicopters preparing to fly food to isolated villages in the mountains during the famine of 1985. The Russians sent $2 billion in military aid to Ethiopia, but almost no food. The grain loaded in the helicopters was part of the $350 million of food and medical supplies sent from the United States.*
ABOVE: *Mothers waiting for antibiotic eyedrops for their babies. Medicines were brought in by American visitors, including the author, at right.*

ABOVE: *Two families outside their homes—made of mud, dung, straw, eucalyptus wood, and the much-coveted tin roofs.*

OPPOSITE, ABOVE: *Inside their one-room house, a mother and child sit on the mud ledge used for relaxing, eating, and sleeping. In the corner are the cooking utensils and the basket and water jug made by the women of the household.* OPPOSITE, BELOW: *The menstrual hut, called "the shelter of blood," is set aside from the rest of the village with a barrier of stones. It is a welcome time for most women* to rest from their labors. Some feel like queens, as relatives come to visit and bring food. ABOVE: *The synagogue in Weleka where Ali-tash and her family worshipped. On the Sab-bath, no one cooks or draws water. Sex is forbidden, and even circumcisions, pros-cribed for the eighth day after birth, are post-poned to Sunday.*

OPPOSITE, ABOVE: *Dressed for Shabbat: the mother in her white shamma, the daughter in an embroidered dress, the father and sons in western clothing.* OPPOSITE, BELOW: *Inside the synagogue in Weleka young men wrap themselves in prayer shawls brought by visitors from the United States and Israel. Framed on the wall is the famous 1973 letter from the* Sephardic Chief Rabbi of Israel, Ovadia Yosef, proclaiming once and for all that the Falashas are Jews. ABOVE: *To protect the villages from guerillas and bandits, a number of Jewish men are given rifles by the government. Here they are inside the synagogue in Ambober.*

OPPOSITE, ABOVE: *The interior of the Ambober Synagogue with the Ark and the table for reading the Torah.* OPPOSITE, BELOW: *Young people preparing to welcome the Sabbath.* RIGHT: *A village beauty in Ambober, the largest Jewish village in Ethiopia.* BELOW: *A newcomer in Israel praying in the Orly Hotel in Netanya.*

ABOVE: *Ethiopian children romping with Is-raelis and children from other lands in the Na'Amat Day Care Center in Ashdod.*

BELOW: *In Israel, after work, a father plays with his sons, who are bathed and well-fed, and all in their new Israeli clothes.*

The emperor looked puzzled.

"Who is in charge of these students?" he asked the minister of education.

"Yona ben Naftali."

"Yona! Where is Yona now? It is years since I have seen him."

"Your Highness, he sits outside this door."

"Bring him in."

Yona entered and bowed his head. He too did not kneel to touch his face to the floor.

"How are you, Yona?" the emperor asked.

Yona guessed he had been forgiven. "I am well, Your Majesty."

"What can you do about these children? I offer them jobs and houses and they talk about teaching your people."

Yona looked at the young people he had selected and sent to Israel. Thank God, he thought. Thank God for their strength. They were powerless young people; the emperor had absolute power; and yet they had the courage to say no to him.

"Your Majesty," Yona began. "Do not think them ungrateful. They know well the value of what you are offering them. But, Your Majesty, they have prepared themselves for years to fulfill a dream. A dream to teach Falasha children how to read and write. Your Majesty, someday perhaps they will come back to Addis and take up your kind offer. But now, I ask you, allow them to go to our villages in Gondar and Tigray, allow them to open the doors of learning to our children."

The emperor was angry. "You have no land! Jews have no land! Where will you build schools?"

Yona answered politely. "Your Majesty, we will make agreements with the Christian landowners. We will rent land in the villages and build schools on the rented land."

Emanuel hardly heard Yona's answer. He felt something tugging at his pants. He looked down; it was the emperor's little dog. Without bending, Emanuel flipped the side of his trousers, trying to wave the dog away. To no avail. The dog pulled on his pants, then stopped, perched himself on Emanuel's shoe, peed a warm yellow stream, and trotted off to run between Yael's legs.

A flunky hurried across the chamber with a silk cloth and wiped Emanuel's shoe.

Emanuel could concentrate again. He heard the emperor snap at Yona, "Do you think they will succeed?"

"Indeed, Your Royal Highness. They will succeed because they are imbued with passion. They will be teachers, bringing wisdom and knowledge to our villages. They will succeed because they have a cause, Your Majesty, a great cause—to impart what they have learned to their brothers and sisters."

Haile Selassie turned full face to the young people. In his low voice, he said, "I warn you. Instead of going forward here in our country—after all that you have seen and learned in Israel—you are going to go backward."

The young people stood tall and straight and silent.

"Go with your teacher, Yona." The emperor dismissed them. "Now you are filled with eagerness and devotion. Later on, you will be disappointed and give up. You will fail."

They left the throne room, assuring one another outside the palace that the emperor's prophecy would be unfulfilled.

IN THE NEXT years, Yona became the representative of the Jewish Agency in Ethiopia, supervising the village schools, buying supplies, paying the salaries of the teachers. Philanthropic American and English Jews also sent money for the schools.

More of the young people returned from Kfar Batya and they too became full-time employees of the Jewish Agency. They earned sixty birr—thirty dollars a month—and lived, like all the villagers, in straw tukuls or mud huts, with no plumbing, no electricity, and dirt floors. They did not complain; they were performing a holy task; they were teachers stretching the minds of young children. They were proving the emperor was wrong.

In Ambober, the largest of the Jewish villages and with the largest school, Yona sat proudly listening to Emanuel teach. Twelve hundred students, trudging on foot from the neighboring villages in winter cold, in rain and mud, came to the Ambober elementary school. Classrooms could not hold them all. Often Emanuel taught forty and fifty pupils under a tree. In the evening, in his mud hut, he talked with his teacher Yona.

"Yona, we are revolutionizing a whole generation," Emanuel said. "Before you sent us to Israel, the *kess* was the teacher. He could only teach religion, and even that he taught in Ge'ez, not in Hebrew. He didn't know Hebrew. It was a kind of closed learning. We're changing everything, breaking the norms, changing concepts, changing thinking. We're teaching them everything—history, math, Hebrew. I tell them, 'Education is the key to our future. Without education, we will never grow.'"

Yona nodded.

"When I can't teach them any more," Emanuel went on, "I tell them, 'Go to the government high school in Gondar.' Yona, their parents are afraid to let them go. You know that in the days before we went to Israel, when Jewish children left the villages to study, they went to mission schools and we lost them. So now the parents are against us. They say to me, 'You are destroying our children. You are sending them to government schools where they will be called *buda* and they will be persecuted.' Some of my students go to the high school and hide that they are Jews. But they must go and learn. I tell them, 'I have been in the Holy Land. Now you, and all the community, you are going to Israel. The day of redemption has come. I am preparing you for *aliyah*.'"

BUT THERE WAS no *aliyah*.

The Foreign Ministry had vested interests in Africa. Surrounded by hostile neighbors, Israel desperately needed friends. In the late 1950s, she began her own "Peace Corps" program, eagerly teaching other developing nations what she had learned by trial and error. The Africans trusted her. Thousands of Africans came to study free in her universities and medical schools. African friendship became a cornerstone of her foreign policy, and there were some who argued that rescuing the black Jews of Ethiopia now might rock the boat.

No more students were invited to Kfar Batya. After three years, Yona closed the school in Asmara and returned to Addis.

In 1960, Emanuel knocked on Yona's door in Addis Ababa.

"May I come in?" Emanuel asked.

"You are always welcome." Yona led Emanuel to the sofa. "Will you have something to eat? Coffee? Tea?"

Emanuel shook his head. "Yona, I've resigned from the Jewish Agency. I can't teach anymore."

Yona, shocked by the anguish in Emanuel's face, heard the emperor's prophecy, *You will be disappointed and give up.* "What happened?"

"I feel I am a liar. I see myself morally ruined. I have confused the children in my classes, and I have confused their families. I promised them they would go to Israel, and they are not going. My integrity and my dignity are destroyed."

"No, no, Emanuel. You mustn't say these things about yourself. You are one of our best teachers. The children love you. The children are hungry for what you can give them."

Emanuel seemed not to hear. "What are they waiting for in Israel? Why are they waiting so long to save us?"

"Listen to me, Emanuel. I don't know the answer. I too thought by this time many of us would be in Israel. Someday it will happen. Believe me, it must happen. But now . . ." Yona raised his arms in frustration.

The African wind sent a sudden chill through the living room.

The distraught young teacher sat holding his head in his hands. "I can't go back. I can't stand up in a schoolroom and lie to the children."

"You're not lying to them. In a country like this, it's a holy mission teaching children to read and write."

"It's a holy mission only if you believe what you're teaching. I don't believe it anymore. I can't be a teacher any longer. I know how important it is to teach the children to read and write. But I was teaching them also about Israel. Now I think we'll all be dead before they take us in. Why are they waiting? Oh God, why?"

Yona put his hand on the young man's shoulder.

"What will you do?" he asked softly.

"I'll find some kind of job here in Addis."

"Whatever you do, my door is always open to you. I'm sure you'll have no trouble finding work."

Yona was right. Fluent in both Amharic and Hebrew, Emanuel became the liaison agent for a construction firm. Haile Selassie had invited Israeli firms and architects into Ethiopia. They were to help modernize his land. They erected government buildings in his capital. They built an asphalt road from Addis to Gondar. They put up a sports stadium and constructed hangars in the new Bole Airport in Addis. They were bringing Ethiopia into the new world.

Emanuel earned $140 a month, nearly five times as much as he had earned as a teacher. He lived in a villa with a bathroom and indoor plumbing, with floors that could be scrubbed, and electric lights. He even acquired a car and a mistress.

For nearly five years, Yona lost touch with him. Then on a warm evening in 1965, he opened his door to find Emanuel, smartly dressed like a European in a silk suit, waiting.

"Praise God," Yona exclaimed. "Where have you been? What have you been doing? I thought I would never see you again."

The two men embraced and kissed.

"Something is wrong," Yona said.

"You can tell?"

"I've known you since you were a little boy. Come in."

Emanuel followed him into the house. They sat facing each other. "I'm a rich man, Yona, but a confused one."

Yona listened in silence.

"I was once very religious, as you know," Emanuel said.

119

"But here in Addis, I went to live among the Christians and I got lost."

"It's never too late—" Yona began and stopped.

"My mother and father were so afraid I would marry outside the faith, they walked for three months down the mountains to Addis to talk to me. My mother took ill on the way, but she came. She had to make sure I was still her son, the son she had been so proud of, the son who had seen Jerusalem."

Yona stood up. "You will never betray her."

"I'm quitting my job. Five years is enough. I'm going back to Israel. I have to find out why the government and the Jewish Agency have forgotten us."

A FEW MONTHS later, Emanuel was back in Yona's living room, impatient and angry.

"As soon as I arrived in Jerusalem," he told Yona, "I began knocking on doors, asking everybody, 'Why have you forgotten us?'

" 'I don't know,' they said. 'Go ask somebody else. Go find your answer in another office, not here.'

"I argued with the leaders of the government, with the Jewish Agency, with anyone who would listen. 'It's a life and death struggle,' I told them. 'We have to get the Jews out soon or they'll be finished—hunger, famines every few years, war and persecution. We're now about thirty-five thousand Jews. If we don't leave soon, the whole community will be wiped out.'

"But Yona, nobody would listen. President Ben-Zvi is dead. President Shazar is obsessed with saving the three million Jews of Russia, and surely you heard what Yisrael Yeshayahu, the speaker of the Knesset, said."

"I know." Yona had been outraged when he learned that the Speaker, a Yemenite, had advised the Ethiopian Jews to convert to Christianity. That, he assured them, would solve all their problems.

"I asked them in Israel," Emanuel went on, "how can the Rabbinical Council and people in the government argue that we're not Jews when for hundreds of years we were persecuted and killed for our Jewishness? Long before the Romans conquered and destroyed Jerusalem, we were Jews obeying the laws of Moses. I quoted Amos to them, 'Are ye not as the children of the Ethiopians unto Me, O Children of Israel? saith the Lord.' 'Do you know,' I said to some of the Russian and Polish Jews, 'Ethiopia appears ten times in the Bible. Poland and Russia not once.' "

"And no one listened to you." Yona's voice was tinged with bitterness. "They're still arguing whether we're descendants of the ancient Ethiopian Agau tribe or the Lost Tribe of Dan."

"What is it, Yona? Is it something evil?"

"I can't believe that."

"Is it our color?"

Yona shrugged his shoulders. "They've taken in brown Jews from Yemen, yellow Jews from Afghanistan, black Jews from India. I think the people are ready to accept us, if only some of the people in the government will end their debate."

"I tried to tell them that in Israel. I said, 'If we don't save our people now, we'll lose them forever.' "

Despair clouded Yona's face.

"Haile Selassie doesn't want us to leave," Yona said, "and Israel is in no hurry to take us in."

YONA PACED HIS courtyard, tormented.

Why indeed were they delaying the rescue?

For, on a government level, relations between Haile Selassie and Israel had never been closer.

Yona watched the emperor walking a tightrope. He was the Christian ruler of a half-Christian country in a sea of Arab states. Yet, cunningly, with little publicity, he had brought in a host of Israelis.

Israeli doctors and nurses healed his people. Israeli farmers and fishermen taught his peasants modern techniques. Israeli professors lectured in English in his Haile Selassie I University in Addis. Israeli officers trained his army and police. When his empress, a severe diabetic, needed hospitalization, he sent her to the Hadassah Medical Center in Jerusalem.

But emigration for the black Jews, dreaming of returning to Zion, was forbidden.

AFTER THE Six-Day War in 1967, Emanuel returned to Israel, joined a kibbutz, entered the army, and continued to fight for the rescue of his people.

In one of his letters, Emanuel told Yona how he had helped two men of power form the Public Council for Ethiopian Jews. One was Professor Aryeh Tartakower, a writer and professor of sociology at the Hebrew University. The other was the colorful Ovadia Hezzy, born in Yemen and raised in Aden, the highest-ranking sergeant major in the Israeli army. He sported a walrus mustache, disported himself like an English officer, and was famous for having converted into Hebrew the English marching commands, "Hup, two, three, four. Hup, two, three, four."

Eagerly, Yona read how the two men had gone to see Pinchas Sapir, the no-nonsense boss of the Jewish Agency.

"You must do something for the Falashas," Hezzy had told Sapir.

"What do you want me to do?" Sapir asked.

"Bring in four hundred to five hundred a year."

Sapir was sympathetic. "But," he asked, "what do we do if we can get out only two hundred a year?"

"Any number," Hezzy said decisively. "But start now."

Sapir brought the issue to the government. The debate in the government and among the Orthodox rabbis became heated.

Hezzy and Tartakower had no patience. Hezzy prevailed on his good friend the Sephardic chief rabbi, Ovadia Yosef, to announce once and for all that the Falashas were Jews.

In 1973, the rabbi made the historic pronouncement in the form of a letter to Hezzy, a letter in his own handwriting.

Emanuel sent a copy of the letter to Yona.

Dear Mr. Ovadia Hezzy, precious friend and man of great action, may peace and salvation be yours. . . .

My decision, in my humble opinion, is that the Falashas are Jews whom we are obliged to save from assimilation and whose return to Eretz Israel we must expedite. . . . To save a single Jewish soul is to save an entire world.

Could anyone now question their Jewishness? Surely, now the *aliyah* could begin.

But still the government did nothing.

The Law of Return did not yet include the Jews of Ethiopia.

YOM KIPPUR, 1973. Egypt's President Anwar Sadat invaded Israel.

The Arab oil potentates skyrocketed the price of oil. At the same time, they prevailed on the African states to break all diplomatic ties with the Jewish state. In return, the Arabs promised the Africans they would not suffer. The friendship with the Africans that Israel had so carefully nurtured was shattered.

Haile Selassie succumbed to the pressure. He closed the Israeli embassy and forced most of the Israeli teachers and farmers, physicians and builders, out of Ethiopia.

Yona fell into despair. The exit doors to Israel were sealed tighter than ever.

But the Arab potentates reneged on their word. They gave no concessions to the Africans and the price of oil kept soaring. Ethiopia's fragile economy was shaken; its agriculture declined, the world demand for coffee—its main export—fell. And a devastating famine swept across seven provinces of the land.

By the end of 1973, it was estimated that 3 million people were affected and 250,000 had died.

Haile Selassie's regime was tottering. He had ruled the country like a medieval potentate from the time he had become the Regent Ras Tafari Mekonnen in 1916.

To most of the world, he was a romantic, gallant figure who had stood up against Mussolini; exotic, sensitive, with his dark beard and brooding eyes, his slaves fanning him with huge palm leaves, protecting him from the Ethiopian sun with a scarlet and purple umbrella glittering with sequins.

Yona knew him as a different man, a demogogue, a theatrical monarch concealing his lust for total power with rhetoric and gestures. Both miserly and corrupt, he fostered corruption in the palace's labyrinthine politics. It was said that he had deposited hundreds of millions of dollars in Swiss banks. While most of the populace was starving and illiterate, his courtiers were building palaces and sending their fortunes out of the country. Civil and political rights were unknown, free elections unheard of. People suddenly disappeared. Political opponents were arrested, imprisoned, and tortured in barbaric, festering prisons. For political and criminal offenses, the emperor imposed the death penalty, usually without trial.

Jews, barred for 350 years from owning land, had not only to give Haile Selassie the 10 percent tithe all peasants paid him and bring half or more of their crops to the landlords, but pay high rent for the land they farmed as impoverished sharecroppers.

Strikes erupted among the peasants and workers, who earned little more than a hundred dollars a year. Students demonstrated. Revolt against the emperor was in the air. A middle class had begun to emerge. They too began to turn against the emperor.

The famine of 1973 and the unrest doomed him.

At first, Haile Selassie ignored the famine. After all, people had been dying of hunger in Ethiopia for centuries. Then he tried to conceal it, but the world learned of the catastrophe and an international outcry drove him to take some action. He decided to visit some of the devastated areas. The presence of the King of Kings, Elect of God, Descendant of King Solomon, Lion of Judah, His Unrivaled Majesty, His August Majesty, His Most Exceptional Majesty, His Most Puissant Majesty and Distinguished Highness would surely comfort the dying and silence his enemies.

He still had loyal followers who adored him, convinced he had the magical powers of divinity. As he traveled with his retinue of princes, bodyguards, cooks, pillow bearers, valets, and maids, starving peasants poured white paint on treeless rocks and drought-deadened soil to hide the devastation from the royal gaze. Hungry mothers combed the hair of the dying children they carried to the roads to catch their last glimpse of the emperor.

It was too late. His mishandling of the famine fueled the political fires.

His army mutinied. In June of 1974, officers in the army and police created the Dergue (*dergue* is an Amharic word for "committee"). It was the coordinating committee of the armed forces, the police, and the territorial army.

While the emperor wandered inside his garden feeding his favorite lion and his panthers, the Dergue was rounding up his aristocrats and noblemen, imprisoning his ministers and his courtiers, arresting even the royal family until almost no one was left in the palace with the old emperor but his trusted valet. Prisoners, thrown into jails, were tortured and hanged.

The Ethiopian calendar is different from the calendar used in most of the world. In the Ethiopian calendar, September 12, 1974, was New Year's Day. Before dawn, a group of junior officers in combat uniform burst into the palace, forced the emperor to listen to a proclamation of deposition, hustled him into the back seat of a green Volkswagen, and drove away.

The Lion of Judah, King of all the Kings of Ethiopia, disappeared into the old palace in the hills above Addis Ababa.

Some of his children fled to safety; others waited in basements and jails to learn their destiny.

One of his great-granddaughters, Esther Selassie Firknes, found haven in Jersey City, New Jersey. She was seventeen when the Dergue drove off with her great-grandfather.

"The official word given to our family," she told me, "was that the emperor had died of the complications of old age. But his daughter, who was my great-aunt, and her daughter went to see him two days before he died. He was in the old palace under house arrest. It's true he was psychologically depressed, hopeless about the situation. But they found him physically well. He was eighty-two and appeared to be ten years younger. He never drank, never smoked, and was so disciplined that people marveled at how careful he was in what he ate.

"That was why they were surprised, two or three days later, to be told that all kinds of medical complications had happened and he had died. They were told a doctor had seen him, but my family could not find this doctor to verify it. My gut feeling is that he was murdered. Nobody ever saw the corpse. Nobody knows where he is buried."

The country was now in the hands of the Dergue and the newly formed PMAC—the Provisional Military Administrative Council.

The PMAC promised "a revolution without bloodshed." But the revolution soon turned bloody. In November 1974, fifty-seven members of the *ancien régime* were shot in cold blood, early victims of the reign of terror and carnage that was soon to follow.

Thousands began to flee across the borders to Sudan, Somalia, and Kenya. Each night the screams of imprisoned families deemed loyal to the emperor pierced the air.

Yona heard how prisoners were tortured by immersing their heads into buckets of blood. Their faces and hair were burned, their legs broken, their genitals shattered by electric shocks.

Israel decided to try to extricate the Jews from the chaos of Ethiopia.

In 1974, Koor, Israel's largest industrial complex, sent a representative to Ethiopia with contracts to recruit seventy people to work in Israel. After weaving his way through the Byzantine bureaucracy, he succeeded in bringing out seven young men. Unfortunately, a press conference broadcast in Israel made the Ethiopians aware that he was recruiting only Jews.

No more Jews were brought out with contracts to work in Israel.

The next year, the Jewish Agency tried another route.

Every night, thousands of Ethiopian Christians and Moslems, escaping the famine and the revolution, were crossing neighboring borders into Kenya, Sudan, and Djibouti.

The agency would try to rescue Jews through Kenya.

Twenty-eight young Jewish men traveled across the country. They reached the border only to be caught by the Ethiopian border patrols, arrested, and tortured.

In 1977, a pivotal year in the lives of the Ethiopian Jews, the Israeli government decided it had one realistic option: direct negotiations with Lieutenant Colonel Mengistu Haile Mariam. A series of dramatic events triggered this decision.

In February, the thirty-four-year-old Mengistu, after a bloody shoot-out among his rivals in the Dergue, had become the all-powerful chairman of the PMAC.

Until now, Ethiopia had played a strategic role in American foreign policy. The United States had sent vast amounts of arms and economic aid. The U.S. Army had built a sophisticated communications center at Kagnew Station on the outskirts of Asmara, the only such electronic listening post in all of black Africa, with a military garrison of thirty-five hundred Americans.

In February, President Jimmy Carter, incensed by the violation of human rights and the reign of terror, announced that further military aid would be drastically reduced.

In retaliation, in April the Dergue shut down all U.S. operations except the American embassy and the Agency for International Development. Four days later, Washington stopped *all* arms shipments to Ethiopia.

A month later, some two thousand high school and university students were murdered in the famous May Day massacre. Yona's son was one of the few who escaped.

That same month, Israeli elections brought Menachem Begin to power. Soon after, he agreed to meet with the leaders of the Ethiopian community. He listened, totally absorbed, as Emanuel and David, the son of Yona, described the plight of the Jews in Ethiopia. Begin's whole family had been murdered in the Holocaust. These young Ethiopians struck a chord. He realized, he told Emanuel and David, that "the Falasha community is one of the most ancient in the Jewish dispersion, *and we must bring them home.*"

ETHIOPIA WAS NOW at war with Somalia, on its eastern border, and the war was not going well. The Soviets were arming the Somalis heavily. Mengistu was desperate for replacements for his American equipment.

Learning that Begin was to meet with President Carter, Mengistu sent a message asking Begin to intervene on Ethiopia's behalf. Begin grasped the opportunity but failed to convince Carter, who refused to resume sending arms to Marxist Ethiopia.

But now Mengistu, in need of military replacements, agreed to a deal. Israel would sell Ethiopia arms. In return, Mengistu would allow Jews to leave. The deal was kept top-secret.

Begin made his decision. The Ethiopian Jews were to be repatriated. In August, an Israeli air force plane landed at the airport in Addis Ababa. Fifty-nine Ethiopian Jews, many in rags, walked onto the tarmac and hurried aboard the plane. Among the fifty-nine were Yona's youngest son Isaac, and his son Jeremiah, who had escaped the May Day massacre and now came straight out of hiding.

In December, a second Israeli plane landed in Addis to carry sixty-two more to Israel. The young people dubbed the two aircraft "the ammunition planes"—guns for Jews.

Yona was exultant. "Tourou," he confided to his wife, "a hundred and twenty-one people have now flown to Israel with no danger to their lives. It's all legal. We'll be able to get thousands out this way. Maybe we can save our whole community."

But three months later, in February 1978, Moshe Dayan, Israel's minister of foreign affairs, was asked by reporters at a press conference in Switzerland, "Is it true that Israel is selling arms to Ethiopia—a Communist satellite?"

Obviously, the secret had been leaked. Dayan said simply, "Yes."

Mengistu was caught red-handed. In the Arab and Communist worlds, few deeds were considered more heinous than trafficking with the "Zionist entity."

Now the world, especially the Arab world, knew that Mengistu was getting arms from the Jewish state and allowing Jews to leave—young men who might later join the Israeli army and fight the Arabs. Abruptly, he canceled the airlift.

"Never explain and never apologize" was the motto by which Dayan, an enigmatic figure in Israeli politics, had lived his life.

Later, in a short debate in the Knesset about Israeli arms to Ethiopia, Dayan replied that Israel had sent arms to Ethiopia in the past, but no longer. "I told the truth," he said.

But there were some who argued that saving the black Jews of Ethiopia was not on his agenda.

In 1978, the new Ethiopian government introduced a series of reforms. Rural and urban land was nationalized. The holdings of the wealthy landowners were broken up. Peasants were given small plots of land to till for themselves. Even some

Jews were given small plots of land and the promise of a better life. For a few months, it seemed as if the lot of the Jewish
community would really improve under the revolution.

But reform and terror, in the nature of revolution, went
hand in hand. Murder became a ritual. And the Jews became
easy targets.

Some landlords refused to give up any land to the Jews who
had so long been their sharecroppers. Associations of peasants
and urban dwellers were formed to function administratively
at local levels. The peasant associations shut their eyes when
the Jews were refused land or given the least tillable patches
of soil. Jews were forced to get permits to travel from one
peasant association to another. Escape from the villages became more dangerous than ever. Angry landlords burst into
Jewish villages and engaged in incredible acts of torture and
cruelty. They murdered and castrated men, raped women,
amputated children's feet, bound old people to trees and bushes
to die, and sold captives into slavery.

In the next weeks and months, Yona, waiting in Addis,
received anguished letters from his children in Israel. They
described how the Ethiopians in Israel were meeting in each
other's homes in a communion of agony. Had their parents,
their sisters, their brothers survived the massacre?

Finally, out of their pain came action. They would no longer
accept the mandate of the government and the Jewish Agency
leaders who warned them, "Jews can be saved only by silent
diplomacy. Publicity can kill more people than we can save."

"Silent no more," the Ethiopians shouted. "Silence is the
enemy."

In February 1979, they came by car and bus and truck. They
came from Beersheba and Ashdod and Safed, they came from
the Galilee and the Negev to Jerusalem.

They were no longer the shy, soft-spoken Jews of the mountains and the desert. Dressed Israeli-fashion in faded denim
and jeans, in skirts and cotton blouses, in sandals and sneakers, shouting their slogans, they marched past pine groves and

rock gardens up the winding hills of Ruppin Road toward the wrought-iron gates of the Knesset.

Here they sat, chanting their call for action. TV and still cameras caught the anguish in their faces. Young people told reporters how their families were suffering in Ethiopia, and how they themselves spent days and nights weeping, fearing their parents were dead. Many Israelis learned for the first time that 350 Ethiopian Jews were living among them. And some now joined their struggle.

A week later, Prime Minister Begin met with Emanuel and Yona's son David, and with Rahamim Elazar, who had come in the early 1970s and was the first Ethiopian Jew to graduate from any university in Israel.

Desperate and tormented, Emanuel pleaded: "Mr. Prime Minister, we can't wait. Our people are dying. They're being robbed, murdered. Too much time has passed already. Save them!"

"We want to save them, but how do you propose we can do it?" Begin asked.

"We can bring them out to Sudan through the Armachiho Forest."

"What!" Begin exclaimed. "I hear that forest is filled with bandits and wild animals. The worst people live there. If murderers and gangsters run away, they hide in that forest."

"You have heard the truth, Mr. Prime Minister." David spoke with passion. "But so much do the Jews of Ethiopia long to come to Israel, they are willing to go through that forest."

Begin sat for a while in silence. Then he said, "The government of Israel will not give an order, nor will it advise the Jews of Ethiopia to come. But should they cross the dangerous Armachiho Forest and arrive in Sudan, then the government of Israel will take responsibility."

Begin promised he would again appeal to the Ethiopian government to let the people go.

But Mengistu's government was no longer amenable.

Months passed. Small groups of young people, slipping out of Ethiopia, trekked through the Armachiho Forest, crossed the desert in Sudan, and reached Israel. But the numbers were insignificant, and the fears for their families so painful that those in Israel grew desperate.

In October, the Ethiopian leaders organized another demonstration. They had learned a lesson well—demonstrations brought out the press, and the press was on their side.

Begin, still faithful to his promise to rescue the Jews, appointed an interministerial committee to work on the problem and coordinate the activities of the government and the Jewish Agency. He himself was the first chairman.

The committee met once a week, and worked closely with a newly formed group in America called the Committee on Ethiopian Jews, part of NJCRAC, the National Jewish Community Relations Advisory Council.

Several times a month, NJCRAC received a secret list of the numbers who had arrived safely in Israel and shared it with all the agencies and people involved with the Ethiopian Jews. The information was to be disseminated orally, but was not to be published or broadcast.

Meanwhile frightening stories filtered out of the refugee camps in Sudan. Overcrowding, hunger, and disease were decimating the people.

Again the Ethiopians in Israel met with Prime Minister Begin, who promised once more to help.

No ONE KNEW that help would come in the wake of Camp David.

On March 26, 1979, on the lawn of the White House, Menachem Begin, Anwar Sadat, and Jimmy Carter signed the Camp David Peace Accords.

With peace now in sight, Begin directed the Mossad to speed up all efforts to bring the Jews of Ethiopia home. The Mossad had a long history of secretly smuggling Jews out of Hitler's Europe.

In iron-clad silence, enlisting Emanuel and other former Ethiopians, the Mossad began the rescue by land and sea and air.

Some of the people were picked up by planes on hastily built desert runways.

Some, driven to Sudanese ports, climbed onto ships that sailed the Red Sea and in forty-eight hours set foot on the soil of Eilat. Several were even rescued by submarine.

Some were flown in small chartered craft to Kenya and from there to Europe and Israel.

And in the fall of 1979, the Ethiopian government agreed that Yona, Tourou, and their daughter Judith could travel to Israel to attend the family "wedding."

Yona went again to his Christian friend Abebe. "I have my chance. Finally, they are giving us permission. Are you sure you still want to be my guarantor?"

"Absolutely, Yona," Abebe said. "You are my good friend."

"I will understand if you want to change your mind," Yona said. "You know the risk you are taking."

"You must go, Yona. Nothing will happen to me."

Tourou and Judith's guarantors, whose identities must still be kept secret, also agreed to take the risks. Yona was told they must return in three months or their guarantors would be jailed.

Airfare to Israel was beyond their resources. David turned to Graenum Berger, the founder of the American Association for Ethiopian Jews who arranged for the AAEJ to pay for their flight.

At Ben-Gurion Airport, a delegation of young Ethiopians, surrounded by journalists, photographers, and television cameramen, cheered the travelers as they stepped off the plane.

The reporters threw questions at Yona. Deeply moved by the reception, he described the murders and the torture of thousands of people.

The interview was flashed by news services around the world. It reached Mengistu's government. A friend in Addis called Yona at his apartment in Petah Tikva.

"You must never come back," his friend warned him. "Your life is in danger."

Yona gasped. "What about Abebe, my guarantor?"

"He has already disappeared."

"You must find him. Nothing must happen to him. He has a family. Children. You can't let him be harmed."

"Yona, we think he is dead."

The telephone fell from Yona's hands.

BOOK THREE
Operation Moses

Chapter Nine

NOT EVEN THE sun rising feverishly over Ethiopia's deserts and mountains could change the color of windblown dust. Old and feeble men and women crawled across the dead land searching for a blade of grass or a glimmer of water. Dying babies sucked their mother's empty breasts. Children lost their childhood.

The terrible famine of 1984 swept across twenty-six countries of Africa, a haunted wind that struck death to everything that lived.

Fourteen-year-old Ezekiel, long-limbed like an Ethiopian Olympics runner, with a sensitive child's face, left his little village south of Gondar with his parents and his sixty-year-old hunchbacked grandfather.

They were to join two hundred others trekking to Sudan. Their leader was a Christian guide who demanded one hundred birr for each adult and sixty birr for each child. It was more than most peasants earned in a year. To raise the money, Ezekiel's father, forty years old, a strong and skilled farmer, sold their cow, their ox, and the loom on which he wove the cloth for their shammas.

In their tukul, they bade farewell to relatives and friends, kissing them countless times on both cheeks. "Come soon to Jerusalem," Ezekiel's young mother Rachel whispered to her family.

Ezekiel saw his mother's body convulse in a fresh spasm of coughing. In her hollow eyes was the unspoken fear that she would never see her parents and her relatives again.

For weeks she had been coughing blood. In all their region, there was no doctor. "You will get better in Jerusalem, Rachel," Ezekiel's father assured her. "Doctors there will cure you."

In the middle of the night, they slipped out of the hut, carrying the little food they had on their backs. Outside their village, they joined the procession of two hundred Jews, and began the trek that would take them two hundred miles to Sudan.

Ezekiel had heard how Christian guides often robbed the people on the way and disappeared. He thought grimly, our guide has no reason to rob us. We have nothing.

It was the tenth year of the famine that had helped depose Emperor Haile Selassie. The drought was still sweeping across sub-Saharan Africa, causing more havoc in Ethiopia than in any other African land.

The revolution, the drastic changes in agricultural policies, the war with the rebels on the political left and the landlords on the right, had added to the famine's devastation. Forests had been chopped down for firewood. Roots holding topsoil had disappeared. In the heavy rains, rivers of water raced wastefully down the eroded hills, leaching the soil of minerals. What earth there was had vanished. Rocks were now the terrain. They walked across a wasteland that looked like craters on the moon.

They were but three days into the trek when Ezekiel's mother Rachel collapsed on the ground.

A strange sound gurgled from her throat. Ezekiel lifted her ravaged body.

"Mother," he cried.

Her hands fell lifeless at his side.

The procession halted while Ezekiel and his father placed her on a bare rock, covered her with stones, and stood silently while a *kess*, escaping with them, recited the prayers of comfort for the dead.

At home, Ezekiel and his family would have sat on the ground for seven days of mourning. Now there was no time. He closed his eyes to say good-bye. They were deserting her with not even a tree to shade her body. Above them, birds of prey wheeled in the sky.

After the first week, Ezekiel's hunchbacked grandfather Moshe could no longer walk.

"Leave me," he pleaded with Ezekiel and his father. "I will die peacefully. Don't hold the others up. Save yourselves."

Ezekiel hoisted him on his back.

"No, no, I'm too heavy" his grandfather protested even as his legs began to dangle over Ezekiel's shoulders.

Ezekiel and his father took turns carrying the old man until after a few hours he said, "Let me down now. I am stronger."

Ezekiel found a stick to help his grandfather walk.

A month later, of the two hundred who had left in the dark of night, some one hundred reached Sudan and entered the camp of Um Raquba. All the others had died.

Um Raquba, a city of despair when Alitash and Daniel had taken refuge there in 1980, was now in 1984 a city of death and dying. More than twenty thousand refugees from Ethiopia were huddled together, divided into two areas, the Jews in one area, the Christians and Moslems in the other. Of the twenty thousand, some eight thousand were Jews.

Inside the camp, an earlier arrival directed them to the far end of the camp. "That's where the Jews are," he said. "Go quickly, and then try to stay out of sight."

"Food," Ezekiel said, "Where is food?"

"There is no food today. Go find some place to sleep. Maybe there will be food tomorrow."

Lifting his grandfather once again on his back, Ezekiel trudged beside his father to the far side of the camp where the Jews sat in the dark of their tukuls and tents.

A man standing at the entrance to a tent beckoned them to enter. "We will make room for the three of you," he said.

Some thirteen others sat apathetically looking at the new-comers as Ezekiel lowered his grandfather to the ground. The hot sun sent a shaft of light into the darkened canvas tent.

Ezekiel's grandfather and father stretched out to sleep, but Ezekiel sat wide awake. Around him were gaunt, despairing mothers holding shriveled babies in their arms, too weak even to cry. On the ground lay older children with distended bellies, bones protruding through their sunken cheeks, limbs thin and lifeless.

Quietly, Ezekiel talked with the man who had invited them in.

"In Ethiopia we heard there was food in the camps in Sudan."

"There is food here sometimes," the man answered. "The United States sends food. Europe sends food. Private relief groups send food. But much of it is piled up on the docks in Port Sudan on the Red Sea. Either they don't have enough trucks, or the roads are bad, or they can't keep up with all the people who just keep coming in. Between the famine and the food rotting on the docks and no medicine for all the diseases, every day twenty, thirty, fifty, sometimes a hundred people die. It's like a death watch."

Ezekiel looked apprehensively at his grandfather, curled up, lying exhausted on the tent floor. Even his tall, strong father seemed spent.

"When we entered the camp," Ezekiel said, "someone told us to stay out of sight. What did he mean?"

"He meant what he said. Stay out of sight. The Christians and Moslems in the camp know someone is helping us get out of here. They hate us."

"They hate us for that?" Ezekiel was bewildered.

"They're jealous. They can't get out. No country will take them. People do terrible things when they're jealous. At night, if we don't protect ourselves and stand watch, they come into our tents. They rape our women and murder our men. Be careful, I tell you."

"Why did thousands of you come now?" another man in the tent, who had arrived earlier, asked him. "Was it the famine?"

Ezekiel answered thoughtfully. "It was not the famine; we have known starvation and famine before."

He paused, remembering the sense of wonder and urgency that had swept the village. "Each day we sat in front of my grandfather's tukul and talked and talked. My grandfather said, 'God is telling us to go to Jerusalem. The way Isaiah told it in the Bible, that we would 'rise up with wings as eagles.'

" 'If we don't go now,' my grandfather said, 'we will suffer and be punished.' We knew then. It was the time to go."

FOOD ARRIVED the next day.

Ezekiel hurried to the line, where he was given rations for three adults—flour, powdered milk, edible oil, and peas. He filled a can with water. Outside the tent, he built a fire, prepared the food, and fed his grandfather, then he and his father slowly savored what was left.

During the night, his father woke, writhing in pain. He shook Ezekiel to wake him.

"What is it?" Ezekiel asked in alarm.

"I am dying."

"No, no, Father," he pleaded. "Father, don't die. I need you."

His father heaved a sigh of pain and wrapped his arms around his bloated stomach. He crawled out of the tent to vomit the food he had eaten. His body shook with diarrhea.

In the morning, Ezekiel raced through Um Raquba searching for a doctor. He found a Swedish nurse in one of the relief stations. They hurried to the tent.

But Ezekiel's father was already dead.

"I'm so sorry," the nurse said, and walked slowly back to the relief station.

In his despair, Ezekiel turned to one of the men in the tent. "Why did he die?"

The man placed an arm around the boy's shoulder. "Who knows? It could be the water. It's bad water. It could be something in the food. It could be some disease."

"Why did he have to die before we reached Jerusalem?"

"Maybe it was not his destiny, like Moses. Moses too did not live to enter the Promised Land."

Ezekiel and his grandfather sat motionless and silent in their grief. Then Ezekiel rose and made a shroud of his father's tattered shamma. Two men fashioned a stretcher from sticks they found in the scrubland. They helped Ezekiel place his father on the stretcher and carried him to the graveyard on the mound behind the camp.

In the desert camp that had become a city of dying and death, he said good-bye.

Now only he and his hunchbacked grandfather were left to make the journey to Israel. How much longer could his grandfather hold out? Would they survive the diseases that were killing hundreds every day? Would Sudan allow them to stay until rescue came? And most of all, would the rescue come in time?

IT WAS A tradition in Africa to grant haven to people in flight. True, refugees were dependent upon the U.N. and private international agencies for food. But it was African culture, African hospitality, to give the homeless land and allow them to stay.

Sudan, Moslem in the north and Christian in the south, was a natural haven for Moslems and Christians. But Ethiopian Jews moving through Sudan created a sensitive issue.

In 1979, the problem had become so acute that Prime Minister Begin met urgently with his experts on Africa. What did they foresee? Would Sudan change its time-honored policy of humanity? Overflowing with people, would it arrest the hundreds of Jewish refugees and force them back to Ethiopia, to possible torture or death?

The following year, under orders from Prime Minister Begin and working under a blanket of silence, the men of the Mossad began to move small groups along the underground route that Alitash and Daniel had followed. "My boys," Isser Harel, the head of the Mossad, said of his secret agents, "make so-called heroes like James Bond look like amateurs."

At the same time, the American Association for Ethiopian Jews (the AAEJ) brought twenty-one Jews from Sudan to Germany. Five settled in Germany, one committed suicide, and 15 were brought to Israel.

Impatient with the rescue, the AAEJ began attacking both Israel and American Jewish leaders for doing nothing. Yehuda Dominitz, the director general of the Jewish Agency's Department of Immigration and Absorption, was singled out, accused of dragging his feet.

Dominitz was a man in turmoil, respected and loved by some who regarded him as a compassionate social worker, attacked by others as a taciturn bureaucrat. Tragedy was etched into his face. His parents and his two younger brothers had been murdered in Auschwitz. He himself had been saved by Youth Aliyah in 1939 when, as a thirteen-year-old, he had fled his native Czechoslovakia. For three decades, he had been involved in rescuing Jews from Europe, Asia, and North Africa. Now, though policy was made by the government, he was being pilloried, committed to silence while the Mossad was secretly rescuing groups like Alitash and Daniel's and flying them to Israel.

RESCUE IS A metaphor for survival. Rescue creates its own heroes. Rescue inspires unlikely men and women into life-saving.

In 1983, an American to be known only as Jeff, successful in both business and the arts, slipped into Sudan. Swiftly, he hired people to work with him, calculating it would cost three thousand dollars to rescue each man, woman, or child. He and his cohorts began moving individuals and small groups through Juba in the south out of Sudan into Nairobi in Kenya.

If there was a sense of high adventure in his work, there was also a brooding sadness; sadness for the deaths lost in the Holocaust, sadness for the dying in the camps in Sudan and the terrible cost in human life.

A market in false passports had grown up in Africa, masterminded mainly by refugees from Eritrea, the stretch of land in Ethiopia along the Red Sea. With money forwarded to him by the American Association for Ethiopian Jews, Jeff and his people bought passports, airplane tickets, paid for hotel rooms, and whisked little groups of people on planes to Europe and then Israel. Several times his wife, an American who had served as a nurse in the Haganah before Israel was born, became the tour leader. The AAEJ announced that Jeff had rescued some one hundred refugees.

Meanwhile the Mossad was secretly rescuing thousands. Unhampered by censorship, the AAEJ bought ads in the *New York Times*, and the Anglo-Jewish press asking for contributions and continuing to decry Israel and the American Jewish establishment for doing nothing to rescue the Jews.

Israel's ambassador to the United States, Meir Rosenne, was besieged. "Are these ads true? Why is Israel not saving the Jews of Ethiopia?" The ambassador and his aides were close-mouthed. Silence was the imperative.

In Jerusalem, Prime Minister Begin told his interministerial committee, "I'm ready to have everybody accuse me of doing nothing if, by saying one thing that might glorify me, I might harm a single Ethiopian Jew."

Moshe Gilboa, director of Jewish affairs in the Foreign Ministry, was bitter. "While we're trying to save the Ethiopian Jews, we're being viciously attacked. There are two reasons why Ethiopian Jews are coming here now. First, they dared to remain Jews for all these centuries of suffering. And second, Israel opened its doors and its heart to them. The ingathering of the exiles is the raison d'etre of our existence. Whoever betrays that betrays the essence of the establishment of our state."

In the tug of war, of publicity versus secrecy, a battery of committees sprang up. In America, a new organization called the North American Conference on Ethiopian Jewry (NACOEJ) was founded in 1982 by Barbara Ribakove, then a medical writer, to help in the rescue and absorption. NACOEJ, less adversarial than the AAEJ and working quietly, was able to cooperate with the Jewish Agency and the Foreign Ministry in Jerusalem. In Israel itself, the Ethiopians formed some ten different committees. To end the confusion, the government formed a committee to coordinate all the Israeli committees. It was called The National Council for Ethiopian Jews in Israel.

Rescue was the top priority. Africa was starving, but Israel, of all the nations in the world, sought to save lives by bringing the people into its own borders.

Generously, the United States poured hundreds of millions of dollars in food and drugs and cash into Ethiopia and Sudan for the sick and hungry. But the U.S. immigration quota for all of Africa was twenty-five hundred a year.

Canada, slightly less restrictionist than it had been during World War II, accepted only professionals and technicians who could fill the gaps in Canada's economy.

Sweden, more humanitarian than most, invited only handicapped people, unwanted by other countries, to come, perhaps even to be healed.

But Israel took in every Jew, crippled or blind, strong young men and women, parentless children, old and often broken people who would never be able to care for themselves.

By the end of 1983, over seven thousands Jews had reached Israel. Sudan was still overrun with refugees. But in the camps, there were virtually no Jews left.

THEN SUDDENLY, as 1984 dawned, some ten thousand Ethiopian Jews rose up and left their ancestral villages. Ezekiel and his family were among them.

With their shammas wrapped like prayer shawls around their heads, looking like Jews of the Bible, they trekked across Ethiopia toward the Promised Land.

Tens of thousands of Christians and Moslems were now fleeing the famine and the Marxist government, taking refuge in the chaotic Sudanese camps. Hundreds of refugees died each day. But the death toll of Jews climbed higher than that of any other group.

In the Um Raquba camp, Ezekiel saw the fear that helped kill them. Fear of picking up rations, lest they be noticed, though they were starving. Fear of going for medicine when they were sick. Fear of acknowledging they were Jews lest they be murdered. Married women were less vulnerable to rape, so single women married men they scarcely knew. Parents arranged quick marriages for their twelve- and thirteen-year-old daughters, hoping marriage would protect them.

"The conditions I saw in the camps were terrible," Emanuel, who had earlier rescued Alitash and Daniel, told me later. "In one of the camps, I saw worms living in the water. Our people brought a chemical from London, and some pills. The chemical purified the water, so we gave the people the good water to drink, and then the pills to cure them. But do you know what preparation and money it took to bring those chemicals and pills into Sudan? And the risks? And trying to

146

keep the people alive, so we could save them? And still they kept dying. In Um Raquba, I saw a mother holding her dead child, a two-year-old little girl, in her arms. She had been holding her for four days. She said she wanted to give her a Jewish burial in Jerusalem."

Each day fourteen-year-old Ezekiel trudged up to the mound behind the camp, carrying the bodies of those whose painful trek had ended in the fetid heat of Sudan.

In the early months of 1984, one thousand Jews died.

Still, nothing could stop the exodus. Thousands more left their villages, trekked to Sudan, hid from other refugees, and dreamt of Jerusalem.

By the summer of 1984, more than ten thousand Ethiopian Jews were once again overflowing the camps of Sudan, struggling to stay alive.

IT WAS CLEAR to Israel that only a massive airlift, like the Magic Carpet Airlift that had rescued the Jews of Yemen in 1949, could save the Ethiopian Jews stranded in Sudan.

But such an airlift could be undertaken only if Sudan agreed. Egypt's President Sadat was dead, assassinated because he had dared to make peace with Israel. Israel and Sudan had no diplomatic relations. No Israeli emissary could go directly to President Nimeiri. His regime was already shaky; his political opponents, the Moslem Brotherhoods, whom he had nicknamed "the Brothers of Satan," would have made political capital the moment they discovered he was trafficking with Israel.

Only the United States could help. In the continuing, often desperate East-West struggle for power in Africa, Nimeiri was now in the American camp. Israel turned to the State Department.

Forty years earlier the State Department had consistently barred refugees fleeing Hitler from entering America. A 1944 Treasury Department report called "Acquiescence of this Government in the Murder of the Jews" had been an impassioned denunciation of the State Department. "One of the greatest crimes in history, the slaughter of the Jewish people in Europe," the government report had charged, "is continuing unabated." Officials in the State Department, it said, "have not only failed to use the Governmental machinery at their disposal to rescue Jews from Hitler, but have even gone so far as to use this Governmental machinery to *prevent* the rescue of these Jews."

The year 1984 saw a different breed among State Department officials.

One of the pivotal figures was Howard Eugene Douglas, Jr., generally known as Gene, who bore two titles: U.S. coordinator for refugee affairs and ambassador at large.

"I'm determined," he told me in Washington, "to show that there are people in the State Department today totally different from the State Department of World War II."

A friendly cosmopolitan from Wichita Falls, Texas, Gene Douglas was a commander in the U.S. Naval Reserve; a linguist fluent in six languages; a conservative Republican close to the inner court around President Reagan; a Protestant determined to rescue Ethiopian Jews.

"I believe in the continuity of life, in the human link in history," he explained his commitment. "I was commited because of my own memories as a four-year-old in the hard, rough country in Texas, sitting on the porch listening to my grandmother tell me of her life. It was because of my own four-year-old son Christopher. And mostly it was because of the Ethiopian Jewish children. I knew as certain as anything on earth that the Mengistu regime was moving to homogenize the country and deprive Jewish children of their tradition and their birthright. The only way to preserve that tradition was to lift them out of Ethiopia and get them into Israel."

The second key figure was Richard Krieger, the associate U.S. coordinator for refugees, a Bronx-born fifty-two-year-old with graying black hair, and thick black eyebrows. For fourteen years, he had worked as a Jewish Federation executive, and in 1981, after a six-month stint with the Republican National Committee, was invited to join Ambassador Douglas and the Reagan administration. A maverick in the State Department, he could be soft-spoken or strident, courteous or demanding, diplomatic or aggressively firm, and always pragmatic.

Douglas and Krieger, operating the office of the coordinator for refugee affairs, were political appointees. They made policy; they had no funds to carry out their policy.

A second refugee office in the State Department, called the Bureau for Refugee Programs, held the funds. Under its director, James Purcell, the bureau distributed the millions of dollars Congress appropriated for such refugee organizations as Catholic Relief Services, Save the Children, HIAS (Hebrew Immigrant Aid Society), the International Red Cross, and especially the United Nations High Commission for Refugees (UNHCR), the agency most responsible for supplying food and medical care to the people huddled in the overcrowded camps of Sudan.

Both refugee offices and both directors, Douglas and Purcell, who frequently disagreed on policy and tactics on other issues, were totally committed to rescuing the Ethiopian Jews.

A fourth figure, a career diplomat in the State Department, must still remain nameless.

These were the men, working with the Israelis, who helped put the pieces of the mosaic of rescue together. Parts of the mosaic must still be concealed in the hope that more may be saved.

THE SUDDEN exodus caught the United Nations High Commission for Refugees by surprise.

In his office in the State Department, Richard Krieger described the failure. "The director in Sudan was Nicholas Morris, an Englishman born in Sudan. Reports reached us that Morris had difficulty relating to the Ethiopian Jews. He couldn't understand their problems, their customs, their religion, their diet.

"All the refugees suffered," Krieger went on, "but the Jews suffered more than any of the others. There was plenty of food on the docks in Port Sudan, sent by world food organizations, but it didn't get to the people. Hundreds died of starvation and malnutrition. There were tremendous parasite infections."

Over lunch, Krieger continued the inside story of bureaucratic failure. "Why didn't they preplace food or medical supplies at Sudanese camp sites? They said the food and medicine would become magnets and draw more refugees. In reality, they refused to take the necessary actions and thus were responsible for most of the deaths. The AAEJ reported 'death tolls as high as twelve-to-fifteen hundred,' figures we were able to corroborate later."

In Um Raquba, a Swedish nurse, Elizabeth Broberg, arriving in May 1984, described her first sight of the Jewish refugees "lying all over the place. There wasn't enough shelter. There wasn't enough food. We had very little medicine. The people were afraid of medical care, they didn't want anything to do with it. Some of them practiced bloodletting. Then came the measles. It was incredible how many died."

Anders Maltson, a male nurse also from Sweden, decided to alert the U.S. Embassy in Khartoum. He found Jerry Weaver, a 250-pound Midwesterner, working as refugee coordinator in the Bureau for Refugee Programs.

In the State Department, Weaver was regarded by many as bright but frequently undisciplined and of questionable judgment, a cowboy who loved to hunt big game, a stereotype of the "ugly American." But Weaver knew Sudan. According to Gene Douglas, "he was there when we needed him. He had a streak of romantic adventurism that can produce extraordinary achievements, or monumental disasters."

In boiling heat, Weaver set out from Khartoum, driving south and east some 250 miles to Um Raquba to see for himself.

He entered the tents and tukuls, horrified by the sights and smells of people huddled in rags. Trusting no one, the Jewish refugees hid their sick and dying children.

"The situation was appalling," Weaver told a correspondent of the *Los Angeles Times*. "We talked to the people and they said, yes, probably as many as three or four or five hundred people had died. No one knew how many. We visited the clinic, the one the Swedes worked out of, and they didn't have any medicine. The supplementary feeding program was without food. Walking through, it was obvious there were a lot of people just not eating. You could see it. Also, it was raining, so the sanitation situation was just horrendous, because the Falasha would not go out of their tukuls, and some of these huts contained as many as ten, twelve, fifteen people. The Swedes told us, and the Commission of Refugees told us, and the Ethiopians told us—it was just impossible to get the Falasha to come out. They were terrified."

Back in Khartoum, Weaver described the agony of Um Raquba in a cable to the State Department in Washington.

Krieger, associate coordinator for refugees, shot off a blistering cable to UNHCR headquarters in Geneva demanding to know what the agency was doing in Sudan and asking for corroboration of the Weaver and AAEJ reports.

The UNHCR replied more conventionally. They would send one of their people from Geneva to investigate and at the same time ask Morris for a more detailed report of his activities.

Their investigator reported that conditions in the camp were not critical; food and medicine were plentiful; the death rate was normal.

The deputy head of UNHCR in Geneva, Richard Smyser, an American and a former Foreign Service officer, then queried Washington. How could their investigator's report have been so totally different from Weaver's?

Weaver was ordered back to Um Raquba. He discovered that the UNHCR's investigator had never gone to the camp but had relied, he said, on "informed sources."

Douglas and Krieger were outraged. A meeting was arranged between Krieger and Smyser who had come to Washington. Smyser promised that UNHCR would start immediately to provide adequate food, medical care, and shelter.

The problem, Gene Douglas told me, "was not with the UN high commissioner, Poul Hartling of Denmark, nor with Smyser, the deputy high commissioner. Both these men were well aware that this was a program of importance to the U.S. Government, a program of extreme humanitarian concern.

"As in most agencies of government, the problem lay at the working level. The agency itself had become sluggish, bureaucratized. On its staff were people of little moral courage and rigid prejudices working in an area of human suffering that required high moral courage and compassion. The bureaucrats insisted that helping Jews who were in desperate shape was not their business."

THE WASHINGTON afternoon sun streaked through Douglas' windows in his office as he worked at his desk, waiting for Krieger to usher in a Sudanese diplomat.

Covering the entire wall behind Douglas' desk was a handsome map of the world. The map was symbolic. Refugees were scattered across Africa, the Middle East, the Far East, Latin America. In 1984, refugees stretched across the globe.

Douglas bolted out of his chair as the Sudanese diplomat, who must remain nameless, entered and greeted him with a hug and a broad smile.

"Welcome, my friend," Douglas said, leading him to the opposite end of his office. A brown leather sofa flanked by two brown leather armchairs defined the office. It was the domain of a strong masculine executive.

"Do sit here." Douglas waved the Sudanese diplomat to a corner of the sofa, and then seated himself in the chair next to the sofa. Krieger sat in the opposite chair.

Like a stage director, Douglas had carefully arranged this seating plan for all his visitors. He wanted to be close so he could lean toward them as he spoke, and if they came from a culture of "touching people," he could touch their arm or hand as they rested it on the bend of the sofa.

The Sudanese perched on the edge of the couch. He was dark-skinned, of medium height, with intense black eyes, a corpulent body that spoke of good living, and eloquent hands which he used constantly.

"Eugene," he said in flawless English, "things are very serious in the Sudan. You know what a poor country we are and how we are struggling to improve the life of our own people. The refugees are a burden to the Sudan and while we have received generous assistance from our friends, it is not enough." He flailed his hands in the air. "The Sudan is losing ground, Eugene." He repeated the words like a lament. "Eugene, the Sudan is losing ground."

Douglas leaned forward. "We are old friends. You know my affection for your country and my respect for you and what you are trying to do. Let us talk frankly."

"Indeed."

Douglas went on. "There are two distinct refugee situations in the Sudan, not just one. They require different approaches to resolve them. In the south are the refugees from Uganda. In the east are the Ethiopians and the Eritreans. Let's agree for the moment to leave the Ugandans and the Eritreans out of the discussion and talk about the Ethiopians. Within the Ethiopian camps, we have the special problem of the Jews. You know they're there. I know they're there. *Other people* in the region know they're there." "Other people" was a euphemism for Israel. Thus Douglas guarded their friendship. If, when the Sudanese reported his meeting with Douglas, he should be asked, "Did you talk about Israel?" he could answer truthfully, "We never even mentioned the word."

Douglas continued. "I have the sense that the number of Jews is growing to a level that can no longer be dealt with under current methods of transportation. What do we do?"

The Sudanese diplomat moved his head forward and back,

nodding in African Moslem style. "Yes, yes, go on. What do we do?"

Krieger spoke. "We need to be innovative. We need to conceive a plan so that those who wish to leave Sudan can leave safely without compromising the government or complicating its relationship with the Arab countries in the region."

"Yes," the Sudanese exclaimed, "this is exactly what we need to do." Then he paused for a moment. "Eugene, we need real help. The refugees are one problem, a major one. But, economically and politically, we have other serious problems. The rebels in the south—the Sudanese People's Liberation Movement—they are being supplied with arms from Libya and Ethiopia."

Douglas and Krieger exchanged swift glances. They were well aware of Sudan's vulnerability. Libya's Colonel Muammar Qaddafi had been making thinly veiled threats against Sudan, yearning for it as the gateway to the rest of the African continent. Mengistu too had ambitions of making Sudan a sister Marxist regime.

"We're grateful," the Sudanese diplomat continued, "that Egypt and the United States are our friends. But we are worried. Look what happened to Anwar Sadat. Who knows who is next on the terrorists' list?"

Douglas pressed his friend's arm in sympathy. Nimeiri's regime was shaky. Serious officials in the American government were questioning his grasp of reality. He was only marginally in control. Even his mental stability was in question.

A year earlier, in 1983, hoping to appease the fundamentalists and strengthen his hand, Nimeiri had imposed *sharia*, Islamic law, on the nation. Sudan was now almost as rigidly fundamentalist as the Ayatollah Khomeini's Iran. Common thieves could have their hands chopped off. Prisoners could be crucified publicly and cross-amputated, with one leg and one arm severed. The Christian south was in revolt. Renewed civil war between the Christians and Moslems seemed imminent.

Douglas and Krieger listened sympathetically to their visitor's litany of problems. "You know, of course," Douglas said, "we have no funds in this office. But I promise you I will talk with others in the State Department. I know how serious the crisis is in your country."

The Sudanese diplomat rose. "Eugene, tell them the Sudan is losing ground. Losing ground, Eugene."

Krieger escorted him out of Douglas' office and into his own to talk in general terms about the camps and the problems presented by the Ethiopian Jews.

The diplomat left. Krieger returned to Douglas, his face flushed with excitement.

"Gene, I have an idea. Let me talk to him again. With all the other problems he has, he should be thankful if we help him get the Jews out of those camps in Sudan."

Douglas agreed. "If you can get permission from Chet [Chester A. Crocker, assistant secretary of state for African affairs], and from Hume Horan [U.S. Ambassador to Sudan], then I'm all for helping him get the Jews out."

Krieger hurried through the State Department to get the answers he needed. He went first to Assistant Secretary Crocker, who gave him his approval. Next he found Ambassador Horan, who was in Washington on State Department business. "All right, but be careful," Horan warned. "Don't do anything to jeopardize our relations with Sudan, or anything that will negatively affect the Nimeiri government." Krieger then went across the hall to the diplomat who was to become a key figure in the rescue and who must still be anonymous. Enthusiastically, the diplomat approved the plan.

Krieger returned to his own office, telephoned the Sudanese official, and invited him to return that same afternoon. At 5:30, they sat facing each other in Douglas' office.

Krieger began the conversation. "I want to talk to you about the Falashas."

The Sudanese diplomat, seated on the leather couch, nodded silently.

"Sudan has a tremendous number of problems." Krieger spoke

evenly, but his words were underlined with a hidden passion. "We understand this. You need assistance from the United States government. You need positive help and positive imagery for Sudan on Capitol Hill and in world public opinion. You don't need crazy Americans and Canadians running around Sudan trying to help the Falashas and causing problems. You don't need ten-to-twelve-thousand Jews mixed in with your country's ongoing conflict between the Moslems and Christians and with thousands of other refugees, creating new problems."

The Sudanese diplomat leaned forward nodding his head. "Yes, yes, it's true."

Krieger said, "Let them go. Help them leave. And let me tell you what will happen if you do."

Choosing his words carefully, he offered the Sudanese a rich meal of anti-Semitic stereotypes, reckoning that the more familiar the clichés, however blatantly untrue, the more persuasive they would be.

"You know that the Jews control the U.S. Congress. If the Jews go to the Hill in support of Sudan, think of the aid and assistance you will get."

The Sudanese nodded emphatically.

"You know the Jews control the media. Think of the favorable response you'll get in the press."

Again he agreed.

Krieger continued his outrageous roster of stereotypes. "You know the Jews control the banks. Think how much easier it would be for Sudan to get loans and money."

"It is true."

"At the same time, think of the changing image of Sudan as a great humanitarian country, and how the world will think of *you* as a humanitarian. For all of this, all you have to do is get rid of some people you don't want anyway. We'll work out how to do it if you—"

The Sudanese diplomat sprang from the sofa "You and Eugene are both right. I think we can do it. I'm willing to talk to my people in Khartoum."

At 12:15 the next day, he was back on Douglas' couch. "It's a very good idea. I've already discussed it. I still have to get permission from a few other people, but I'm sure it's something we can work out."

Douglas bent toward the Sudanese. "We both know that there have been some unfortunate instances recently where foreigners [a euphemism for Americans and Canadians] have come into Sudan under false identities, declaring they were relief workers, tourists, or business people. But their true intention was to involve themselves with the Ethiopian Jews."

Krieger added, "If we don't act very soon, these 'crazies' who come to your country to assist the Falashas will create an incident. They could get hurt or killed. Then what would happen? An international incident, terrible embarrassment, and unneeded repercussions for your country. The relations between our two governments will suffer, and make our jobs even more difficult. We must act now to straighten this out."

The Sudanese diplomat nodded.

Douglas now laid his hand on his friend's arm.

"We will need to get the fullest cooperation from your security people, from the apparatus responsible for the security of the camps and the border area."

"Of course. I will discuss it with General Omar el-Tayeb. It must be very secret."

"Be assured," Douglas said, "that we will manage this thing very tightly within our government, involving only the smallest number of people. And we will take no steps here until we too are assured it has been taken up by the right people in Khartoum."

IN KHARTOUM, General Omar el-Tayeb held the key. He was both vice president of Sudan and head of the Sudanese state security police. Next to President Nimeiri, he was the most powerful man in the country.

El-Tayeb agreed that it would be in everyone's best interest to get the Jews out of Sudan. His one condition was complete secrecy. Sudan was a member in good standing of the Arab League. He could not afford to have the Arabs denounce him for allowing Jews to get to Israel.

American Ambassador Hume A. Horan cabled the news of the breakthrough to Washington.

"The U.S. was faced with a delicate political problem," the Washington diplomat who asked that his name be withheld told me. "Our problem was this—how could we facilitate the rescue and still not jeopardize our relations with Sudan—always concerned about its position in the Arab world? A lot of people came together in the department to work out our role.

"People were dying in the camps in Sudan. Suspicion had begun to spread in America that nobody was saving them. People remembered the Holocaust, and the feeling that in those days nobody cared. Was this going to be another Holocaust? They began charging all of us with indifference."

The charges were a painful reminder of the tragic years from 1938 to 1941 when thousands of refugees knocked on the doors of American consulates begging to enter the United States, only to be told, "The quotas are filled." Only later was it revealed that while millions died, less than 10 percent of the wartime quotas were actually filled.

"We couldn't answer those charges." The State Department official shook his head sadly. "The Israelis couldn't answer—they don't put their cards on the table. The Sudanese couldn't talk, or the whole thing would fall out of the water. Yet everyone in the State Department agreed this was a role that was right and was needed. In fact, everything we did was known and approved at the highest levels of government. No one could have done the things we did without the president and Secretary Shultz. But we still had to overcome a lot of obstacles."

DOUGLAS, KRIEGER, and the Sudanese diplomat arranged to see each other in Geneva a few weeks later on the seventh of July. They were to attend the International Conference for Assistance and Relief for Africa.

On July 5, Krieger flew to Jerusalem where he met with three men, Yehuda Dominitz of the Jewish Agency, Moshe Gilboa of the Foreign Ministry, and a third Israeli who must still remain nameless. Krieger described the conversations with the Sudanese to the fascinated Israelis. They savored his story, but told him, "We would prefer to meet directly with the Sudanese."

"Absolutely not." Krieger was adamant. "For you to meet directly with the Sudanese could compromise the whole program. The whole operation can die before it even gets off the ground."

Two days later, Krieger flew to Geneva, where Eugene Douglas and the Sudanese diplomat were playing the game of diplomacy with consummate skill. They met in the company of other delegates. Not a word passed between them about the Ethiopian Jews. Euphemistically, they discussed "the stabilization of the refugee situation in the Sudan."

"Do you trust him?" Krieger asked Gene Douglas.

"Completely. It's this kind of integrity that permits him to serve his government. He's a skillful diplomat, a courageous man, and a patriot."

Behind closed doors, the Sudanese official told Krieger triumphantly, "This thing will work. I just have to iron out a few details."

Three meetings were held preparing the ground rules. Neither the United States nor Israel nor Sudan would breathe any part of the story to the public. This was the key factor. Douglas, Krieger, and the Sudanese agreed as did Yehuda Dominitz, who had also flown to Geneva.

"You still can't meet with the Sudanese people directly," Krieger told Dominitz at a three-way session with Douglas. "But everything appears to be on track."

Dominitz was resigned. "So we won't be able to meet, but let's take care of the main issue—getting them out of Sudan."

"Getting them out of Sudan!" Douglas and Krieger repeated the words almost in tandem. "Then let's get started."

Dominitz returned to Jerusalem, the Sudanese diplomat flew back to Khartoum, and Douglas and Krieger headed for Washington. Krieger and Dominitz arranged to meet again in Geneva in September to work out the logistics of rescue.

SEPTEMBER IN Geneva was golden and peaceful, but the suite in the Intercontinental Hotel had the urgency of a war room.

The State Department was represented by Krieger, James Purcell, the director of the Refugee Bureau, an assistant from Purcell's office, Jerry Weaver, the refugee coordinator, and the American career diplomat whose identity cannot be revealed.

The UNHCR was represented by its deputy director in Geneva, Richard Smyser, and Nicholas Morris, the English-born director for Sudan.

Irving Kessler, executive vice chairman of the United Israel Appeal (UIA), was invited—American Jews would be heavily involved in funding the resettlement of the refugees in Israel. But Kessler, who had undergone surgery, asked Neale Katz, then deputy director general of the UIA in Jerusalem, to attend in his place.

The first order of business was to discuss the appalling conditions in the camps and the reprehensible actions of the UNHCR.

Once again Weaver described the horrendous sights he had witnessed in the Um Raquba camp, the food from the docks that never reached the people, the medicines that never arrived; the contaminated water that killed more people than epidemics, the terror among the Jews of being murdered or raped.

Then, to nearly everyone's surprise, Weaver defended Nicholas Morris, saying Morris had given him valued cooperation.

Morris, still unable to deny the eyewitness account, insisted that the UNHCR had been doing all it could possibly do. Both Smyser and Morris promised that UNHCR would play an increasing role in the camps in Sudan. They themselves would do their best to make sure that food, medicine, and clean water were available. The two U.N. officials were asked to leave. They were not to be privy to the rescue.

The meeting was adjourned and reconvened in the office of an international relief agency whose identity must still be concealed.

Urgently now, the planning began.

The United States and Israel were to mastermind the airlift together.

Israel would begin immediately scouting the world for planes and pilots.

The relief agency would be in charge of moving the people.

The United Israel Appeal, with absolute discretion, would work on getting funds. It was estimated the rescue would cost millions of dollars, the money to come largely from American and world Jewry. In August, the UIA had made a blanket commitment to the relief agency. The American Jewish community would provide whatever funds were needed—no matter what the cost—for food and medical care for all the refugees in Sudan, Jews and non-Jews alike.

Weaver volunteered to coordinate activities on the ground.

The target date was November 4, less than six weeks away.

THEN, ON October 23, 1984, NBC broadcast films of the deaths and starvation in famine-ridden Ethiopia. Photos of children with bloated stomachs and sticklike limbs dying in their mother's arms catapulted out of the TV screens.

The world was aware at last of the famine that had been wreaking havoc for ten years.

Relief agencies were swamped with offers of help and money.

In a few days, Catholic Relief Services received five thousand telephone calls across America from Alaska to Hawaii, pledging donations.

More than $2 million poured into the offices of the American Jewish Joint Distribution Committee to provide relief for all victims, regardless of religion.

Harry Belafonte, the singer and actor, helped launch "U.S. Aid for Africa" and the song that swept the nation, "We Are the World." "I thought we'd get four or five singers and raise four or five million dollars," Belafonte said. "Instead, we got forty-five of the world's greatest artists and raised fifty-eight million dollars."

Schoolchildren donated pennies and dimes to save the victims.

The United States decided human suffering took precedence over ideology. Food and supplies, withheld for years because of Ethiopia's violations of human rights, were shipped again. In October alone, the United States sent eighty thousand metric tons of wheat and other food at a cost of $45 million. The figure would later go to over $350 million.

The Soviets, who had provided their Marxist satellite, Ethiopia, with $2 billion in arms and military aid, finally sent $3 million worth of rice. Soviet helicopters flew the grain shipped from America and Canada to the isolated villages in the mountains.

At the same time, the United Nations decided to build a new convention center in Addis Ababa for $10 million.

And Comrade Mengistu spent $100 million to celebrate the tenth anniversary of the revolution.

MEANWHILE FRANTIC organizational meetings were taking place in Washington, Geneva, and Jerusalem.

To coordinate the actions in Washington, Douglas and Krieger met with Israel's ambassador to the United States, Meir Rosenne, and Robbie Sabel, the embassy's political counselor. Their meetings were reported in memos sent directly to Secretary of State Shultz and the White House.

In Jerusalem's national unity coalition government, the rescue plans were on Prime Minister Shimon Peres' desk, while overseeing the whole operation was the former Likud Prime Minister, Yitzhak Shamir, who was now serving as foreign minister.

Shamir had a special relationship with Ethiopia. In his home in Jerusalem, he told me how in 1947, as the leader of the underground Stern Group, with a price on his head, he had been captured by the British, shackled on a prison ship, and incarcerated in a desolate prison in Eritrea. He had broken out of the Ethiopian jail, made his way to Addis Ababa, and managed to get back to Israel five days after it became a nation. Now he confided, "I knew almost nothing about the Ethiopian rescue operation until Mr. Begin resigned in 1983 and I became prime minister. I don't like to know things I am not obliged to know. It's a habit from my days in the underground. But once I learned what was happening, I talked to the Ethiopians here, and told them no price is too great for saving lives."

In Sudan, Jerry Weaver and his associates were frantically preparing for the airlift. One million dollars was injected like a blood transfusion into Sudan's ailing economy. Weaver and his associates bought four buses, five trucks, spare parts for the vehicles, and five hundred metric tons of fuel oil. The fuel, costing $175,000, was safely stored in an abandoned bottling plant in Gedaref. They stocked a warehouse in Khartoum with 250 blankets, bottles of water, and 220 pounds of dried biscuits.

General el-Tayeb was assured that once the operation was over, the equipment and supplies would be a gift to the Sudanese government.

Most of the Jews were in three large overcrowded camps, Um Raquba, Tewawa, and Wad el Heluw. Others were in scattered small communities; a whole group from Tigray was still in refugee camps at the border near Kassala. All of them had to be brought to the airport in Khartoum.

Weaver's men made sure the dirt roads from the camps to Gedaref, and the country's only all-weather road, the

163

Khartoum-Gedaref-Kassala Highway, were navigable. Working often in unbearable heat, they repaired the highway and the roads.

It was obvious no Israeli planes could be used in the operation. Israeli aircraft landing even in the dark of night would alert the world press and break the secrecy. The airlift had to be carried out by a neutral.

Israel chose Georges Gutelman, a fifty-one-year-old Belgian Orthodox Jew who owned a charter company, called Trans European Airways. For years his planes, with the letters TEA painted across the fuselage, had been flying Moslem pilgrims from Sudan and other Arab lands to Mecca. His aircraft, landing and taking off, would raise no eyebrows in Khartoum. Moreover, he had not only commercial but emotional and religious ties with Israel.

El-Tayeb agreed that Gutelman could ferry the people out of Khartoum. But Sudan, wary of the Arab League, could not allow the TEA planes to fly directly from Sudan to Israel. Their manifests had to show a European destination.

One of Gutelman's friends was Jean Gol, the Belgian minister of justice. Through Gol, Gutelman received the permission he needed from Prime Minister Wilfried Martens. The planes would be allowed to make an intermediate stop in Brussels.

The next weeks were frenetic. In Jerusalem, Yehuda Dominitz as director general of the Jewish Agency Department of Immigration and Absorption, and Chaim Aharon, chairman of the department, held day-long meetings with the Mossad, the army, and those cabinet members who would be involved with the refugees—all awaiting the onslaught of ten thousand people.

From Dan to Beersheba and on to Eilat, hotels and unused buildings were cleared out, empty apartments and abandoned school buildings were painted and repaired, and social workers, health workers, eighteen-to-twenty-year-old women soldiers, and veteran Ethiopian immigrants were corralled. The men of the Mossad were mobilized not for war but for rescue. All over Israel, people disappeared from their houses. Even religious people would get calls on Shabbat. "Be at such and such a place." And they would leave for Sudan.

So secret was the operation that most people involved had little idea what others were doing. But all were filled with a sense of urgency. To be a participant in saving lives was a victory over evil, a triumph of the human spirit.

Israel was back in the job of rescue, the job she had been doing for fifty years since Hitler had begun trapping Jews.

ONE LAST STRATEGIC problem remained.

Trustworthy men were needed who could recognize whether the Ethiopians selected for the rescue were really Jews. Some might be impostors or spies.

For days in Israel, thirty-year-old David Yona, the slender and soft-spoken son of Yona ben Naftali, had been interrogated by the Mossad—questioned, examined, studied. He tried to analyze what they were searching to find. They were trying, he decided, to figure out how resourceful he was. How dependable. How smart. How strong. How incorruptible. How swiftly could he make decisions? Would he break if he were caught and tortured? Then one day he was given a ticket and told, "You will be the chief selector." He thought again of the tests as he flew down to Africa. Every cell in his body seemed alive, sensitized. I am an Israeli now, he thought, but I am black and Ethiopian, and it is for this reason first that they have chosen me. My whole life, he thought, has been like a rehearsal before you go out on the stage. Everything my father Yona dreamed, everything I've been fighting for in Israel—to lift our whole community up and rescue it by air— now at last it will happen.

An Ethiopian Jew met him at the airport, and together they drove to Tewawa, the refugee camp on the outskirts of Gedaref. The two men entered one of the larger tents. David stopped at the entrance and stared in silence. Huddled on the dirt floor before him, lit only by a shaft of light, were half-naked men and ragged women, many of them in the curved, strangely graceful postures of bodies close to death. The light fell across arms that looked like branches of dead trees. Children's faces seemed all bones, like pictures he had seen of skeletons.

The Ethiopian Jew whispered to David, "Let's go now. They're terrified, seeing a stranger. We won't be able today to find which ones are Jews."

David spent the next few days carefully choosing the men who would select the people for the airlift. He called the men "travel agents." Silently, he moved in and out of the tents and tukuls in the three refugee camps, making his plans.

"The sick and old," he directed the travel agents, "must be the first to be taken out. Young, strong people will have to wait for later planes even if it means separating families."

It was a delicate operation. The Christian refugees had guns and rifles. They too wanted to get out. If they learned that Jews were able to leave, they could became menacing. He had to work swiftly. There was nobody in the camp to protect the Jews.

The plans were in place; the November 4 deadline had passed. The first Belgian charter was due the night of November 21. That morning David entered one of the tents in the Tewawa camp and announced in Amharic, "Brothers and sisters, I greet you. I am the son of Yona ben Naftali."

Yona's name raced like an electric current through the dark tent.

"I have come to take you out."

The refugees stared at the slim, handsome young man. Could they believe him? they asked each other. They had come through so much already. . . .

An old man in a tattered white shamma spoke up. "He is Yona's son! We must believe him."

The old man pulled his shamma over his head as if he were about to pray. "Remember in the Book of Genesis when Joseph reveals himself to his brothers. They had come to escape the famine as we are now escaping the famine. Remember what Joseph said: *And God sent me . . . to save you alive by a great deliverance.* God has sent Yona's son David to deliver us."

Some of the people murmured prayers of thanks. The travel agents walked among them, talking in hushed voices, telling those they selected what they were to do and where they were to go.

Outside the camp, Weaver waited apprehensively. The four buses he had bought were stored in a nearby warehouse, with Sudanese drivers protected by el-Tayeb's security police.

Hours passed. Finally, in the middle of the afternoon, David walked out of the camp. "It's working. We're getting the people ready now."

Weaver wasted no time. He drove to the warehouse and led the caravan of vehicles to an open field inside the camp.

Slowly, a few people came out of a tent and crossed the field. They looked terrified. Using sign language, Weaver showed them they were to squat on the ground near the buses. A few others followed.

Inside the dark tents and straw huts, people waited excitedly as the selections were made. One of the travel agents placed his hand on Ezekiel's grandfather lying on the floor. "You can go in the first bus," he said.

"My grandfather cannot walk," Ezekiel said.

"Then you will go too, and you will carry him."

Ezekiel bent down. "Grandfather, we are going."

The old man lifted himself up painfully. "What did you say, my child?"

"We are going to Jerusalem."

"When?" the old man whispered.

"Now, Grandfather. Now."

The old man moved his lips in prayer.

Ezekiel hoisted him over his shoulders, hastened outdoors, and joined the people squatting on the ground.

Within minutes, a river of people followed them, haggard, disheveled, no shoes, no baggage, their shammas ragged, some on crutches, some on young men's backs, yet moving as though some force, some giant hand propelled them.

The door of the first bus opened. David stood at the door, questioning the people to make certain once again who they were.

Before they could answer, others pushed behind them, climbing the stairs, breaking their way into the buses.

Two hundred fifty refugees piled into the four buses. At six-thirty, with dusk beginning to settle, the convoy left the open field.

In the dark, the lead bus took the wrong path. After some confusion, the vehicles turned around, returned to the camp, and this time found the main highway west and north to Khartoum. Checkpoints posed few problems. The security police were in control. Five hours later, the convoy reached Khartoum.

Midnight. The buses pulled over to the back entrance of the international airport and waited. Shortly after 1 A.M., the 707 landed. The buses rolled up to the tarmac. The people spilled out. Mothers carried their babies beneath their shammas in pouches on their backs. Nearly naked children clung to adults' hands. Precariously, they mounted the stairs. Inside the plane, kindly Belgian stewardesses helped them fasten their seat belts. A doctor moved among them, prepared for any emergency.

At 2:40 A.M., the engines roared, the plane raced along the runway, and flew into the African sky.

Operation Moses was underway.

It was dawn, November 22. Thanksgiving Day.

Chapter Ten

EVERYTHING ABOUT the plane was strange to Ezekiel, strange and miraculous. The shape—like a bird, or maybe a giant fish. The metal wings. The innards—two long rows of soft chairs covered with wool. He had seen a few planes in the sky, but never chairs covered with wool.

He looked at the people wrapped in their tattered rags and shammas. His own fear and apprehension were mirrored all around him; his mouth felt bone-dry.

Two hundred fifty people were crowded into the Boeing 707. White women in dark blue uniforms taught them to buckle their seat belts, and motioned to mothers to take their babies out of the pouches on their backs and put them on their laps, fearing they would squash the babies against the soft chairs.

The plane raced down the tarmac, then with a roar shot up into the horizon. Ezekiel murmured a silent prayer: "Dear God, don't let it fall down out of the sky."

After a while, the friendly white women brought trays of food. Ezekiel and his grandfather nibbled a little, then both shut their eyes and fell asleep. Hours later, Ezekiel woke as giant wheels ground their way down from the wings, touched the ground. They were in Brussels, away from probing eyes and ears.

They sat inside the plane for two hours in eerie silence. Then once again, they were airborne, and some four hours later were flying over the Mediterranean.

Ezekiel held his breath as he looked down at the coast of Israel, shaped like the big curved knife he used for harvesting his father's crops. The wheels touched down, the plane raced along the tarmac, then braked and taxied to an isolated spot far from the main runways. He watched as a long staircase was shoved into the entranceway. Three men burst into the plane calling out, "*Shalom, shalom. Baruch haba* [Blessed be your coming]."

"*Shalom.*" Ezekiel and his grandfather joined the others repeating the welcome. "*Shalom, shalom.*"

The Israelis helped those who needed help, leading them down the stairs and into four red buses waiting at the side of the tarmac. They carried little children in their arms and took others by the hand. Many of the children, separated from sick and dying parents, had come alone.

Hoisting his hunchbacked grandfather on his shoulders, Ezekiel walked toward the exit door and slowly began the descent.

"Have we reached Jerusalem?" his grandfather asked as they walked down the steps.

It was not Jerusalem, but to Ezekiel and his grandfather, as to most Ethiopians, all of Israel was Jerusalem.

"Yes, Grandfather," Ezekiel answered, carefully setting his foot down on each step. "We have reached Jerusalem."

"Truly Jerusalem?"

"Yes, Grandfather. Truly Jerusalem."

"The Holy City? The Holy Land?"

"Truly, Grandfather."

At the bottom of the stairs, Ezekiel gently lifted his grandfather from his shoulders. The old man knelt on the ground and kissed it. Then he raised himself, his dark face illuminated as he looked up at the sky. "I have won. I have survived. I have been found worthy in the eyes of the Lord."

Once again he bent to the ground and this time scooped up a bit of earth. He tasted it and smiled. "It tastes like *Gan Eden*." The Garden of Eden. Paradise.

A young mother emerged, malnourished, frightened, holding a baby. The needle of an intravenous solution was injected into the baby's skull. The doctor who had traveled with them on the plane walked behind them, his face ashen with exhaustion. A Jewish Agency social worker rushed the mother toward the waiting ambulance.

"Why is the IV in the baby's skull?" the social worker asked the doctor even as they ran.

"It's the only place we could find a vein," he said.

The ambulance sped the mother, the baby, and the weary doctor to Tel Hashomer, the nearest hospital.

Now the others descended and entered the buses. Soon they were driving west to Ashkelon. They pulled up in front of an old-age home run by the Jewish Agency. The elderly residents had been moved to other institutions.

Veteran Ethiopians greeted the newcomers, asking them as they entered the building: "What village are you from? Do you know my mother? My father? Perhaps you met my sister in the camps in Sudan?"

Ezekiel followed the throng into a large room filled with straight-backed chairs and electric lights. He had never seen such chairs and lights. An elderly man looking up at the yellow bulbs asked, "Is it night so fast or is it day?"

Someone motioned to Ezekiel and his grandfather to take

the chairs in the front row. As soon as all were seated, a German-born Israeli social worker with a kindly round face and freckled skin addressed them. He was Micha Feldman of the Jewish Agency.

"Welcome," he greeted the people in Amharic. "We are happy to have you home with us in the land of our forefathers. This means for you the end of the road of your suffering."

The end of the road of your suffering.

Ezekiel glanced swiftly at his grandfather. Then he put his hand to his throat. Pictures of his mother and father lying in different places with no one to mourn at their graves, pictures of their suffering flashed through his head.

He was pulled back by the sight of a man with a small black beard walking swiftly to the front of the room. It was Emanuel, in blue jeans, a blue denim jacket, a white silk scarf tossed around his neck, and a black skullcap.

He too spoke in Amharic.

"Some of you may not be sure yet where you are. You have now arrived in Zion, in the land of Abraham, Isaac, and Jacob."

Several of the people raised their arms toward the ceiling.

"The action you started two years ago, a year ago, months ago, has come to an end. This is the country that your fathers and grandfathers prayed for, prayed that some day you would return to. Now you have come home."

"*Ishi, ishi* [Yes, yes]," some called out. "We have come home."

"In the name of the government of Israel, of the Jewish people, and of the Ethiopian community living here in Israel, we bless you. Just as we have brought you here, so will we bring your brothers and sisters whom you have left behind."

"*Ishi, ishi.*"

An elder with a massive snow-white beard, tightly curled white hair, his body enveloped in his shamma, stood up. The audience turned to him with great respect. His voice penetrated the hall.

172

"It is as the prophets prophesied: *With the help of the Almighty, we will return to Jerusalem.* So now with the help the Almighty and the government of Israel, the prophecy has been fulfilled. We thank you, the government of Israel, and we thank Jews all over the world. Just as Moses took the Jews out of slavery in Egypt into freedom in the Promised Land of Israel, so you have taken us out of Ethiopia to Israel, out of slavery to freedom."

Emanuel applauded with the people. Then he resumed talking.

"In *Pirkei Avot*, the Sayings of the Fathers, it is written: 'He who guards his mouth, guards his soul.' I ask each of you not to tell anyone the route you took, where you came from, and how you arrived."

The audience nodded in silence. "I have a second request," he went on. "Guard your mouth against spreading rumors of who has died. It is very difficult for us, the Ethiopian community in Israel. We don't know who of our families is still alive in Ethiopia; we don't know who will be able to make the journey, and who has died on the way. Sometimes rumors are spread that somebody has died. Somebody meets an Ethiopian who has recently come and asks, 'Do you know if my mother is still alive?' When he sees the look on that person's face, he suspects something has happened. One man in Israel met a newcomer. He asked him, 'How are my parents?' The newcomer said, 'Your parents are dead.' He fainted on the spot."

Looking at the worried faces before him, Emanuel could sense the tragedy of separation that many knew and all feared. One could write the history of Africa, he thought, in separations. In Africa, separation was endemic, like a killer disease. Emanuel had read books describing how for centuries black men and women had been kidnapped by Arab slave runners, torn from their families, chained and starved on the long marches to the coast, shackled and beaten on the slave vessels, then sold in Europe and America like cows or mules.

Now black Jewish families were being torn apart. But this was different. No one was kidnapped. No one was sold into slavery. The people had risen up on their own.

Indeed, he thought, seeing the dark faces of his people, this is the first time in history that thousands of blacks are being brought out of Africa, not to be sold but to be saved.

Still, they too were victims of the African tragedy. Each exodus, he thought, has its own tragedies.

"So I ask you," he implored, "do not tell anyone of deaths on the way. When we know the facts about the deaths, then a group of us will go to the man or woman here and we will sit *shiva* with them and help them with their suffering."

His tone changed. He began to smile again. "Now I will tell you what will happen in the next days."

THE PEOPLE WERE taken to bathrooms. Most had never seen toilets or porcelain sinks or running water. Then they were conducted to a room where they sat on benches at long tables patiently waiting for food.

Food can kill. Israeli doctors had learned this lesson from the Nazi death camps when the liberating soldiers had given the skeletal survivors all their food. Many who had outwitted death by gas chamber died from eating too much too soon.

The doctors now ordered not only small portions but, knowing the intestinal diseases of Africa, said, "No dairy products yet. No fresh fruits or vegetables. Just boiled potatoes, hard-boiled eggs, bread with some margarine and jam, and a cup of tea. That's all."

That first day, Micha Feldman, Emanuel, volunteers, even some who had come on the airlift and could walk, pitched in to help the cook feed the 250 people. Ezekiel too left his grandfather for a little while to help in the kitchen. Then he returned to the table where the people were carefully helping themselves to one egg, one potato, a cup of tea, and a slice of bread. Ezekiel had never seen such bread. A volunteer, walking up and down the rows of tables, taught him how to smear it with butter and jam and then eat it whole, not tearing it apart like his native injera.

After the meal, the people were taken back to the bathrooms and then led down to a basement lined with rows and rows of mattresses. Ezekiel saw his grandfather murmur a prayer, shut his eyes, and fall asleep. But he was too excited. He felt himself soaring out of the mud hut where he was born, soaring through the sky to a big house, bigger than five huts put together, with many rooms, with water that ran out of some silvery thing that you turned, with light that came out of little bottle-shaped glasses hung from the ceiling, and stacks of a strange but good thing people called bread.

The next morning, he was taken to a room piled high with clothing. He stared unbelievingly; he had never seen such riches. He was told to choose brand-new shirts, blue jeans, underwear, and warm blue parkas for his grandfather and for himself. Someone helped them fit their feet into blue and white designer sneakers and knee-high white socks.

Then a young Ethiopian showed them how to turn on the shower. They discarded all their old clothes except their shammas, changed into the new jeans, the sneakers and socks, zippered up the parkas, and wrapped themselves in their shammas. In their clothes, at least, the two worlds had come together.

They breakfasted on an egg, a slice of bread, and tea, then entered a room where young women sat behind long tables, with interpreters beside them. A pretty social worker in her mid-twenties, speaking through her interpreter, asked Ezekiel's grandfather his name, his age, his village, his occupation, and the names of any relatives he might have here. Then she asked Ezekiel the same questions, writing their answers in Hebrew on a long white sheet of paper.

She spoke softly to Ezekiel. "Would you like to go to school?"

"Yes, oh yes."

"I can send you to a Youth Aliyah school, a boarding school where you can study and learn a real skill."

"And my grandfather?"

"No, it is a school just for young people like you."

"I cannot leave my grandfather. We are all that is left of our family."

She nodded. "Then I will send you both to the absorption center in Beersheba. There you will be able to study Hebrew and go to school."

She filled out some papers, and directed them to another room where a doctor examined them. Some had come with tuberculosis, trachoma, bilharzia, and exotic African diseases Israeli doctors had never seen before. The sick were immediately hospitalized. The doctor found Ezekiel and his grandfather malnourished but otherwise in reasonably good health.

The following day they were sent by bus with other newcomers, in their jeans and parkas and shammas, to the desert city of Beersheba, bound for the Beersheba Absorption Center.

The absorption center, called a *merkaz klita*, was uniquely Israeli. It was a kind of haven. Here the Ethiopians spent a year or more—a respite from the famine, from the trauma of the escape, a place where they could study, learn new skills, recover from culture shock, and enter the new world.

More than seventy centers were now strung across Israel from the Galilee in the north to the Negev in the south. Some were compounds of white or gaily painted cottages. Some were apartments in high-rise buildings.

In forty of the centers, as in one of the most beautiful in the country, Mevessert Zion (Harbinger of Zion) near Jerusalem, the Ethiopians lived side by side with newcomers from America, Canada, South Africa, Iran, the Soviet Union.

For this first year, they were the responsibility of the Jewish Agency, in effect of the Jews of America and the world. After that, the government Ministry of Immigration took over, and they began to pay their own way, using the skills they had learned.

Ezekiel's bus headed toward the Beersheba Absorption Center. Once a barren desert outpost, Beersheba was now a metropolis of one hundred thousand people. Ezekiel peered out the bus window, hardly knowing where to stretch his eyes as they swung past shops and markets and factories and parks and the Ben-Gurion University of the Negev, its massive buildings soaring like earth-brown sculptures into the desert sky.

The bus pulled up in front of a compound of two identical high-rise buildings with nearly a hundred apartments. In 1980, the Jewish Agency had rented the buildings from a private contractor to house five hundred Ethiopians who had been secretly flown in and brought straight from the airport.

The Beersheba Absorption Center had become the pilot project, with social workers, teachers, paraprofessionals, and volunteers learning on the spot how to cope with the Ethiopian Jews.

"Welcome, welcome," Malka Elbaum, the motherly, middle-aged director, herself a child of the Holocaust, called out as the people descended the bus.

Ezekiel saw black Ethiopian women hanging laundry out their windows; Ethiopian men were sunning themselves at the side of a playground; Ethiopian children were romping on swings and a slide, racing in and out of stairwells, playing Israeli games of hide-and-seek.

Lifting his grandfather on his back, he followed Malka up a staircase to a bright two-room apartment. "This is yours," she told him. "Look around. Someone will come in a little while and show you how to use the things that are here—the stove, the refrigerator, the bathroom, the electric lights. I will be back later. You can always find me in my office downstairs." She left them to show others where they would live.

Ezekiel lowered his grandfather to the floor. They were in a bright living/dining room, its bare walls sparkling with fresh white paint. A table and two chairs, the only furniture in the living room, made a little circle in front of the windows.

Cautiously, like a voyager on the moon, Ezekiel walked into the kitchen, looked at the strange objects and cabinets, then into the bathroom, and finally into the bedroom, where he saw two cots covered with sheets and blankets, and a wardrobe for their new clothes. The sound of the Ethiopian children singing Hebrew songs came through the window.

He walked back to the living room and joined his grandfather on the floor. They sat silently, in shock.

TWO DAYS AFTER Thanksgiving, the second plane of the airlift, filled again with 250 people, landed in Israel.

Emanuel and Micha Feldman, the Jewish Agency social worker, realized at once that the old-age home in Ashkelon would overflow. They leased the nearby King Saul Hotel and Club, with manicured lawns, lush palm trees, a swimming pool, a sauna, and even a discotheque.

A disco, Micha thought wryly. What better place to welcome Jews from twenty-seven hundred years of isolation.

The owner of the hotel, David Aroni, an Iranian Jew, was one of the "Teheran Children" who, during World War II, had trekked for miles and miles from Teheran to reach the Holy Land. "At last, I can repay what was done for me," he told me. "I was saved by Israel as a child. Now I can help others."

EACH DAY Ora Donio, head of the social welfare division of the Jewish Agency, drove in a minibus to the airport to meet the refugees.

Ora was an ebullient social worker whose grandparents were Americans. Her orders to her staff of social workers were direct: "Be prepared for everything."

One day a pilot told her, "We've brought a baby in a little box. There was no time to bury it in Sudan."

He brought the baby to Ora standing on the tarmac.

"Where are the parents?" she asked.

"I have no idea." The pilot shook his head.

"Is there a sister? A brother?"

"I don't know."

"We will not move the buses until we find someone of the family."

A translator brought a young Ethiopian whose face seemed expressionless.

"Do you have a dead baby?" she asked through the translator.

"Yes."

"How old was your baby?"

"About six months." Hardly a muscle moved in his face. Then he added, "And she had such a beautiful dress."

The words startled her. "Tell the father," she directed the translator, "that I will come to see him in the hotel in the morning."

Ora sent the baby's body to a hospital to await burial, and the next morning found the young father surrounded by his family.

"Do you want to go to the hospital to see your baby?" she asked.

"No," he said, still without expression. "The baby is dead."

Ora was shocked. That evening, she talked to a psychologist who explained to her, "You must understand, the tragedy is so deep in him, he has come through so much, that he is paralyzed. The whole family is paralyzed. They can't cope now. They will cry later."

But not all the refugees hid their feelings or denied them. Meeting a plane a few days later, Ora saw a young man with three small children, four, five, and eight years old, weeping as they descended.

She hurried toward them with one of her translators. "Why are you crying?"

"In the rush," the young father explained through his tears, "my wife was left in the field—in Sudan."

"We will find her," Ora promised.

Messages were sent to David in Sudan. "Find that mother. Put her on the next plane."

Twenty-four hours later, the young mother was reunited with her husband and her children in the lobby of the King Saul Hotel.

Life and death, Ora thought, ride on Operation Moses. On one plane an old man died and in another a baby was born. The Israeli doctor on board asked the mother what she wanted to name her baby.

"There is only one name," she answered. "Israel."

THE LOUNGE OF the King Saul Hotel was Israel's Ellis Island.

It was a bustling, brightly-lit room with people rushing back and forth. Refugees, still bewildered, dressed in Israeli clothes, knee-high socks and sneakers, and wrapped in shammas, waited at the back of the room to be called. Social workers sat behind long tables, translators at their side, questioning the people gently, compassionately, filling out computerlike sheets of paper.

One of Ora Donio's stable of assistants was Elisheva Flamm, a slender, dark-haired, twenty-five-year-old social worker born in Los Angeles. At four every afternoon, after a full-time job as assistant to Yehuda Dominitz, Elisheva traveled for more than an hour to the King Saul Hotel in Ashkelon, interviewed the newcomers, and returned to Jerusalem after midnight.

"Mostly, I'm exhilarated on the way home," she told me. "But often I go home crying."

Night after night, Elisheva heard the stories of starvation, of robberies and rape on the trek, of beloved relatives dying on the way, unable to hide her tears while she recorded vital statistics.

Name? She learned the custom very soon, that in Ethiopia they had no family names. Only their first name and their father's name. Careful not to humiliate them, she told them they could keep their Ethiopian names, if they wanted, or take new ones. She remembered the stories her mother had told her of the way immigration officials in Ellis Island had often changed names capriciously or given new ones—like the name Tony to people who wore tags that said TO NY.

Later, especially as children entered kindergarten and elementary schools, many Ethiopian names, strange and difficult for teachers and classmates to pronounce, were changed to biblical or modern Hebrew ones.

Birth date? Some knew their birthdays. Others reckoned their lives by events like the year Haile Selassie was crowned emperor, 1930, and the year he was overthrown, 1974.

Family members in Israel? Elisheva hoped to help them find relatives who might be scattered in absorption centers from Kiryat Shmoneh to Beersheba.

Education? Many were illiterate, but others had attended village schools. Some 15 percent had finished high school, and of those who had come earlier, nearly a hundred would soon be enrolled in one-year courses to prepare them to enter the universities.

Early one evening, Elisheva helped seat an extended family of fifteen adults and children at her table. She talked with deep concern to two little girls, twelve-year-old twins who huddled close together, their shammas wrapped furtively around orange velveteen sweat suits.

"Did you want to be married?" she asked.

The twins shook their heads shyly. "No," one whispered. "Our parents married us off in the camp to protect us from men."

Gently, Elisheva asked them to accompany her and a woman translator to an empty corner of the busy lounge. Here, away from the crowded tables, Elisheva ascertained that they had never consummated their marriages.

She brought them back to their family, then left the table to find Emanuel and ask for guidance. It was questionable whether some of the marriages in the camps had been performed by rabbis or *kessoch*.

"Can the marriages of these twins girls be annulled?" she asked.

Emanuel stroked his small beard thoughtfully. It was a sensitive issue. The policy was not to impose life decisions on the people, but to help them understand the options open to them. Then the families could make the decisions themselves. Emanuel spoke with the family at length.

"From what I have heard," Emanuel ruled, "I think we can say that these young people really never were married."

Elisheva returned to the table wreathed in smiles. "We will record that you are single children."

The little girls nodded. Their parents nodded too.

"As unmarried girls," she went on, "you can stay with your parents in an absorption center to which I will send you. You will be able to go to school. You will have a chance to be somebody in Israel."

The two little girls whispered, *"Ishi. Ishi."*

Elisheva then told the two shy young husbands, who were fifteen, that since they were no longer married, they too could spend their time studying.

"Since you came without your parents," she told them, "I'm going to send you to a Youth Aliyah village. It's made up of young people like you. There you'll go to school; you'll learn Hebrew and a trade or profession. Later, if you and these beautiful girls want to get married, of course you can."

"Ishi, ishi," the boys readily agreed.

Elisheva wrote briskly on the printed sheets and handed each one identity papers. They were now citizens of Israel.

That night Elisheva went back to Jerusalem singing.

She was less successful with a fourteen-year-old girl who had been betrothed at nine and married at twelve. Her marriage had been consummated, and she was pregnant.

"I'm going to send you and your husband," she told the frightened child-bride, "to an absorption center together with your family so that you will be close to your mother."

FOR FORTY DAYS, the rescue continued unabated, a plane flying every day except on Shabbat. It was a huge canvas of rescue, a worldwide network of humanity involving the United States, Israel, Sudan, the United Nations, dozens of relief and welfare agencies, and individual heroes like David, the son of Yona ben Naftali.

In Israel, editors and journalists were called to a briefing as tense as a briefing in wartime. They were told the story and warned that a single leak could end the whole operation. They agreed to publish nothing. Military censorship further insured that there would be a total news blackout.

In the camps, busy selecting the people, David felt good. The secret seemed to be holding. He did not know that leaks had begun even before the airlift started.

Back in September of 1984, at the very time that Israel and the U.S. State Department were working out the logistics of the rescue, an article appeared on the op-ed page of the *New York Times*, captioned "Ethiopian Jews Die, Israel Fiddles." The author, Simcha Jacobovici, a young Canadian, the son of Holocaust survivors, denounced both Israel and the world Jewish community for doing nothing.

Two months later, Jacobovici appeared in his native city of Toronto at the plenary session of the General Assembly of the Council of Jewish Federations, the CJF, demanding to be heard. He brought with him a few Ethiopians and some forty Canadian Jews, many of them students with babies in strollers. One of the Ethiopians was Joseph, the teacher who had been tortured and crippled in Gondar. The demonstrators waved hand-printed banners: ACTION NOW.

U.S. Ambassador Eugene Douglas, scheduled to address a later session that evening devoted entirely to the Ethiopian Jews, tried to dissuade Jacobovici from disrupting the meeting. Douglas revealed to him in private that important events were about to take place. Jacobovici refused to listen.

Instead, with a child in his arms, he sat on the floor in front of the dais, demanding a moment of silence for the two thousand Jews who had died on the trek to Sudan. These two thousand, he insisted, could have been saved if Israel and world

Jewry had helped them. The moment of silence was granted, followed immediately by more shouting. For thirty minutes, the president of the CJF, Shoshana Cardin of Baltimore, tried to restore order. "Look at your programs," she pleaded. "We have a whole forum session on Ethiopian Jews called for an hour from now. You will be welcome to speak there." It was no use. She canceled the plenary.

An hour later, two thousand people packed the forum session. Ambassador Douglas gave the keynote address. Speaking like an unabashed Texan, Douglas turned to Jacobovici: "Simcha, as you know, because I've told you, if you will only hold your water for about six weeks, everything will be resolved in our favor."

The press gave the demonstration short shrift. The reporters were honoring the request for secrecy.

Later, riled perhaps by the charges of "fiddling while Ethiopians died," the chairman of the Jewish Agency, Leon Dulzin, "confided the secret" to some five hundred American and Canadian Jewish leaders.

"One of the ancient tribes of Israel is due to return to its homeland," he announced exultantly. "When the true story of the Jews of Ethiopia is told, we will take pride in what we have already achieved in this most difficult and complex rescue operation."

His remarks were kept off the record. But two days later, Dulzin addressed the World Zionist Organization (WZO) in New York, again revealing the "ingathering of a historic, ancient community."

These remarks too might have gone unreported, except that the WZO issued them in a press release with Dulzin's approval.

Two Anglo-Jewish newspapers, the *Jewish Week* in New York and the *Washington Jewish Week*, published the press release and expanded it. On December 11, with the airlift now operating at full speed, the *New York Times* decided the news embargo had been breached if not lifted. Its story, datelined

Washington, revealed: "Airlift to Israel is Reported Taking Thousands of Jews from Ethiopia." The *Times* story was followed by more revelations in the *Boston Globe*, and for several days television networks flashed pictures of anguished mothers and children being treated by kindly doctors and nurses in Israel.

Israeli journalists pounded angrily on the doors of government. The story was being printed and broadcast everywhere except in Israel. When would the censorship be lifted? "Not until every Jew is rescued from Sudan," they were told. "Security is more important than publicity. Lives are at stake."

Despite the leaks, Sudan and Ethiopia took no action to stop the airlift. Newspaper stories, TV reports—these could be overlooked. So long as nothing official came from the governments of Israel or the United States, Nimeiri and Mengistu could pretend they knew nothing.

Israel estimated that the exodus and the first year of absorption would cost $100 million. The goal for the United States alone was $60 million, to be raised by the UJA—the United Jewish Appeal.

On Wednesday, November 28, scarcely a week after the airlift started, three men were on an El Al plane flying non-stop to Israel. They were Martin Stein, a bearded forty-seven-year-old Milwaukee former pharmacist (later to become chairman of the UJA), Alan Shulman, a veteran UJA leader from Palm Beach, and Elton Kerness, the UJA senior vice president who was to plan and coordinate the fund-raising.

They landed at Ben-Gurion Airport at three in the afternoon, were met by officials of the Jewish Agency and the Mossad, and rushed to the cordoned-off military area. The Trans European Airways 707 had just landed.

The three Americans mounted the stairs and entered the plane.

"I had never seen anything like it in my life," Martin Stein told me. "People were gaunt, sick, leaning on the back of the seats in front of them, too weak to stand. Even kids, sixteen and eighteen, were too weak to walk. Of all the two hundred fifty people, not three wore shoes. We helped them down the stairs. Some were in rags, their clothes all ripped. The Israelis covered them with blankets. The sensitivity! Unbelievable!"

He paused. "The only time in my life I was moved like this was when I saw my children born."

That evening the three men sat in the Tel Aviv Hilton. "Now we've seen. What are we going to do about it?"

"We're going to raise the sixty million dollars."

Nine hours later, Martin Stein flew home, followed two days later by the others.

Sunday morning, planes landing at La Guardia Airport brought together the leaders of all the major communities of America and Canada. They assembled at the airport Sheraton Hotel with the national officers of the UJA.

Alan Shulman addressed the morning session. "I have planted trees in the Negev and I have seen the desert grow," he said. "I have seen the elderly living in dignity in Malben [Old Age] Homes. I have seen hope replace despair. But never, never have I experienced something as Jewish as touching another human life, a life reaching out for help."

Several men and women brushed tears from their eyes.

In the afternoon, Martin Stein exhorted them to action. "This is one of the great moments in Jewish history. We're living the Commandments. The Catholics aren't taking the Christian refugees in Sudan to Rome; the Moslems aren't taking the Moslem refugees to Mecca. Only Israel is taking the Jewish refugees, and telling them, 'We're going to bring you into the mainstream of Jewish life, we're going to teach you to read and write and even use computers.' My friends, we don't have many moments in our lives like this. It gives the lie to the United Nations canard that 'Zionism is racism.' "

Each leader rose and announced what the goal of his or her community would be. In the next days and weeks, in parlor meetings and synagogues, an army of lecturers, swearing their audiences to secrecy, described the world's newest biblical exodus with such passion that the Jewish community, which had been responding generously to the agony of all Ethiopians—Christians and Moslems as well as Jews—raised not $60 million but $65 million.

Operation Moses continued unabated.

David reckoned that by the middle of January 1985, the camps of Sudan, still filled with some four hundred thousand Christian, Moslem, and animist refugees, would have no more Jews. Some eight-to-nine thousand Ethiopian Jews, he figured, would all be home and safe in Israel.

THEN THE STORY broke in Israel.

On January 4, 1985, an obscure magazine called *Nekuda* (Point), written by West Bank settlers, published a brief interview with Yehuda Dominitz, the Jewish Agency's director general of the Immigration and Absorption Department.

Dominitz was sure the editors of this almost unknown journal were committed to secrecy. "Can you give any details about the waves of Aliyah from Ethiopia, and how many came last year?" the editors asked him. "And did the famine in Ethiopia accelerate our rescue operations?"

"On this subject," he answered, "you will not hear anything from me. Simply, it is not permitted to reveal any of these things."

Convinced he was speaking off the record, he murmured "Yes" to the question: "Are the majority of the Jews of Ethiopia now in Israel?" He gave no indication of how or when they had come. Dominitz never used the forbidden words: "Operation Moses" or the name most guarded of all—"Sudan." He was sure security had not been breached.

Nekuda published the interview inside the magazine on page 6. The censors failed to catch it. But two Israeli newspapers, choosing to assume that the ban had been lifted, quoted the interview. Reuters picked it up and flashed it around the world.

On January 3, 1985, Prime Minister Shimon Peres called a

press conference in Jerusalem. He hoped, he said, to divert public attention from the "sensitive aspects" of the rescue, and focus instead on Israel's gallant efforts to feed, house, and absorb the newcomers. His effort to divert the press failed.

Rescue was the story, not absorption.

"Israel Has Airlifted 10,000 Ethiopians," the *New York Times* revealed on January 4.

"Bravo, Israel!" the *London Sun* applauded. "A real life adventure to match anything ever dreamed up by Hollywood."

"Israel alone," England's *Sunday Express* declared, "was capable of plucking a whole people from the nightmare of the Ethiopian famine with such brilliant élan."

"When Israel is aroused," the *Sunday Times* noted approvingly, "it knows no frontiers," while the *Guardian* editorialized: "There are no lengths to which Israel will not go to protect its people, as in the raid on Entebbe, or to avenge them, as in the capture of Eichmann. No other country would have had the nerve, and the total indifference to international niceties, to grab many thousands of people from the mountains of East Africa and fly them to another continent."

David, fearful that the publicity might shut down the operation, worked faster than ever. His fears were well grounded. Arab newspapers denounced Sudan's President Nimeiri; Iran accused him of "shamefully collaborating with the USA and Zionism to exploit the famine in Ethiopia to realize Israel's racist designs." In Addis Ababa, Colonel Mengistu claimed Israel was kidnapping his people to sell them into slavery. He demanded their immediate return.

Now that the rescue was exposed, revealed officially by the government of Israel, Nimeiri could no longer shut his eyes. He told the United States, "I am canceling the airlift immediately."

David, heartsick, received new orders from the Mossad men in Sudan. "Choose the people for the last plane as soon as Shabbat ends on January 5."

David entered the camps. Whom should he choose? You, there, you will live. And you, sorry, my friend, not you. You may have to lie here until we can start this thing up again. Or maybe you'll decide you want to get out of the misery of these camps and go back to your village. God knows what you'll find when you get home. No place to live. Your house taken over. No money to start again. The drought and famine are still killing people in Ethiopia.

No one had an exact census, but David believed there were still some nine hundred Jews left in the camps. Three more planeloads, he thought bitterly, and every Ethiopian Jew in Sudan would have been rescued.

IN ISRAEL, fear for wives or husbands, for grandparents left alone and helpless, for children separated by the abrupt halt in Sudan, swept through the Ethiopian community. Prime Minister Shimon Peres tried to assure the Ethiopians that Israel would leave no stone unturned to save their families.

Waiting in Sudan, David walked through the camps. "Help will come again," he sought to console the refugees. The airlift would be resumed. Mothers would once again kiss their children; sons would once again embrace their fathers. The agony of the people was like an iron chain around his chest.

In Washington, one hundred senators, led by Alan Cranston of California and New York's Alfonse D'Amato, signed petitions to President Reagan urging the government to use American influence to rescue the Jews caught in Sudan. Nathan Shapiro, president of the American Association for Ethiopian Jews, rallied influential congressmen to the cause.

The president, easily won over, briefed Vice President George Bush, who was soon to leave for Africa.

On March 7, Bush met with Nimeiri. The Sudanese president agreed to the new airlift on condition that it be carried out rapidly, with a total blackout of news. Any press leaks could overthrow his government. The United States had been withholding $15 million in aid until Sudan could show it was instituting economic reforms.

The $15 million was now released.

THE RESCUE OF the remaining refugees was nearly an all-American operation. Named Operation Sheba for the black queen, it was directed by the CIA and coordinated with the U.S. Air Force, the State Department, the Sudanese security police, and Israel.

In Washington, Israel's Ambassador Meir Rosenne, and in Tel Aviv, America's Ambassador Samuel Lewis were closely involved.

For David, alerted in Sudan, it seemed an act of pure and rare humanity. American planes would carry non-American citizens to a non-American land. When had this ever happened before?

He returned to the camps to bring the glad tidings. Instead, he found bad news. Some of the refugees had begun the trek back to Ethiopia to find relatives and bring them to Sudan. Others were stranded at the borders. Several young girls, including his own niece, had been kidnapped by Sudanese and were hidden by their captors somewhere in Khartoum.

David asked the Americans for a few weeks to search. He was sure he would find refugees hiding out at the borders, and maybe his niece and other young women who had been kidnapped.

"Impossible," the Americans told him. "Things are too critical in Sudan. Nimeiri's regime is shaky. The Sudanese might cancel the whole thing. We have to do the whole airlift in one day."

David found six hundred refugees and brought them to the Tewawa camp. On March 20, he told the refugees, "It is the time."

On March 21, U.S. Hercules planes with food, water, blankets, medicine, and four doctors took off from a military air base outside Eilat. They carried U.S. Air Force men and women, some of them black Americans with special empathy for the black African Jews. Each plane carried a two-man team of Ethiopian-Israelis.

Five hours later, the first C-130 wheeled down on a dirt airstrip eight miles north of Gedaref. Then every half-hour, a plane filled with the remnant of Operation Moses took off, headed east and north, and landed outside Eilat in the Rimon military airport. Prime Minister Peres and U.S. Ambassador Samuel Lewis stood in the desert sun waiting.

The two men entered the first plane. Ambassador Lewis' eyes filled with tears. "This was one of the most emotional days of my life," he told me.

An old man showed the prime minister the precious thing he had managed to save through the whole trek from Ethiopia to Sudan and now to Israel. It was an ancient holy book, soiled and warped, but beautifully handwritten on goatskin in the liturgical language of Ge'ez.

Peres' eyes too grew moist.

"Listen," the old Ethiopian addressed the prime minister, "these are the things of Moses. We have arrived!"

BOOK FOUR
The Present and the Future

Chapter Eleven

Now THE RESCUE was behind them and they were in the
land. Alitash and Daniel, Yona, Ezekiel and his grandfather, all had to be "absorbed."

In 1980, at Ben-Gurion Airport, Alitash and Daniel were
greeted by their friend Emanuel, who had orchestrated their
rescue in Sudan. They hugged and kissed each other's cheeks
rapidly.

"Remember, I promised you in Sudan," Emanuel said, "that
I would see you in Israel."

"You never failed us," Daniel said.

Emanuel led them swiftly through the crowded airport, the
magic portal through which they would enter the new world.

Past immigration control, then past people waiting at carousels to pick up luggage. Alitash and Daniel, Yael and Shmuel, Malka and the others had no need to wait; they had nothing but the clothes they wore.

Outside the airport, Emanuel opened the door of a minibus. "I'm taking you to Ofakim," he said. "It's a development town."

"What's that?" Alitash asked.

"It's a new town for new immigrants. It's in the Negev, not far from Beersheba."

Alitash looked out the window at the broad crowded highway with buses, cars, trucks racing toward the horizon, telling herself it was all real. She was out of Ethiopia. Out of Sudan. She was in Israel.

"You're going to stay in an absorption center," Emanuel explained as they drove south across a desert landscape glowing amber-gold in the late afternoon sun. He stood at the front of the bus talking through a microphone. "You'll be given everything you need—food, clothes, education, even pocket money."

"How do we pay for all this?" Daniel called out from the center of the bus.

"You can't." Emanuel's small black beard seemed to quiver with pleasure. "It's money raised by Jewish people around the world. They send it to the Jewish Agency in Jerusalem, and the agency takes care of you until you know enough Hebrew and can begin to take care of yourselves."

"Some of us already know some Hebrew," Daniel said. "We learned it in the ORT school back in Ethiopia."

Emanuel nodded. "Now all of you must learn it. To survive and thrive in Israel, you have to know the language."

He paused, looking at the faces of the eager young people. "You may wonder why we stress Hebrew so much. You need the language to learn skills, to vote in elections, to read newspapers, to find out what's happening here and in the world. Language is freedom. Without language, you're a hostage, always dependent on others. We want you to become independent Israelis."

Alitash listened, fascinated. She vowed she would learn Hebrew no matter how tough it was. Whatever it took, she would become an *independent Israeli*.

They drove into the little development town of Ofakim, a modest community that had sprung up from the desert. They were given spartan rooms in a low building that served as the town's absorption center.

They spent most of the day in the *ulpan*—where everything was taught in Hebrew. The U.S. Army had perfected the technique in World War II, and Israel had made it the first tool in absorbing a million and a half new immigrants from seventy countries with a babel of tongues.

The *ulpan* demanded total concentration. Classes from eight in the morning to one in the afternoon. All in Hebrew. No explanation of a Hebrew word in any other language. Meanings were explained by gestures and actions. An hour for lunch. Homework. Group meetings. Supper. Then discussions, spelling words out of Israeli newspapers, learning Hebrew songs, and through music and companionship, beginning gradually to feel at home.

Several times a week, Rachel, a woman volunteer, came to teach Alitash and Daniel and the rest of their little group how to live in Israel. She took them to the bank and showed them how people deposited money and wrote checks. She escorted them to the post office. They explored the automatic laundry. The police station. The drugstore. The labor exchange, where people registered for jobs. The supermarket.

Sometimes Alitash slipped away to explore the supermarket by herself. Shyly, she stared at fruits and vegetables she had never seen in Ethiopia, pyramids of fruit that seemed more beautiful to her than precious beads.

The days were filled, but the nights for the young people were long and lonely. Alitash wrote letters home in Amharic. But thus far, there had been no answer. Had the letters arrived? Was her family afraid to write her? Would the letters reveal to the powers-that-be in Gondar that she had disappeared? Were her parents in jail? Dear God, she turned restlessly on her cot, would she ever see them again?

Why did you give her permission? She heard her mother's angry voice, berating her father. *She is my first-born.*

AFTER TWO MONTHS, Emanuel returned to Ofakim. "You've all done so well here," he said, "you're learning the language so rapidly—faster than we dreamed possible—that we don't think you need an absorption center anymore. We're sending you to a kibbutz in the north. It's called Mishmar Ha-Emek. They have a fine *ulpan* there. You'll continue to study Hebrew, and you'll have a chance at learning a lot of different things. It'll help you decide what you'd like to do later."

The young people sat silently in the bus as it sped out of Ofakim, through the Negev Desert, then along the turquoise Mediterranean to the fertile valley of the Emek—the Plain of Jezreel. Here Deborah the Prophetess had defeated the Canaanites. Here King Saul and his three sons had been defeated by the Philistines. Here David had wept for his friend Jonathan in his immortal song of mourning:

> *I grieve for you, my brother Jonathan.*
> *You were most dear to me.*
> *Your love was wonderful to me,*
> *Passing the love of woman.*
> *How are the mighty fallen,*
> *And the weapons of war perished!*

The bus stopped at the entrance to Mishmar Ha-Emek. The little group, led by Emanuel, walked wonderingly through the settlement of white stucco cottages, surrounded by flower gardens, velvety green trees, and furrowed fields once so malarial that the Arabs had called it the Gateway to Hell.

Mishmar Ha-Emek was a nonreligious kibbutz run by Hashomer Hatzair, the left-wing faction of the Labor Alignment. The liberal-minded kibbutzniks accepted the young dark-skinned Ethiopians as they accepted silversmiths from Yemen, merchants from Baghdad, shoeshine boys from Casablanca, doctors and engineers from Moscow, retired schoolteachers from Chicago and New York. They were all Jews who needed to be absorbed.

Classes in the *ulpan* took up their morning. The rest of the day was spent working. Daniel, his sights set on becoming an electrical engineer, was allowed to work in the electrical shop. Alitash was assigned to the kitchen.

The first day, she ran out of the kitchen. She discovered that the meat she was slicing was not kosher.

Slowly, gradually, she learned that people could survive without being fiercely observant. She was grateful that the Sabbath, the day of total rest in Weleka, was special even in this nonreligious kibbutz. Families, dressed in their Shabbat clothes, strolled with their arms around one another; fathers wheeled baby carriages, mothers played on the lawn with their children. Young people cavorted in the swimming pool. Little groups sat together singing to the accompaniment of an accordionist or a fiddler, and motioning to the young Ethiopians to join them.

Often in the evening, kibbutz families invited them into their cottages to watch television programs, listen to the radio, borrow books and magazines, and play with the children.

"It would all be so good," Alitash said to Daniel one evening, "so unbelievably good, if only a letter would come. If only I heard something from home. If only I knew . . ."

Daniel put his arm around her. "Someday mail will reach us. Somebody will come from Ethiopia and bring us news."

AFTER EIGHT months, Emanuel appeared at Mishmar Ha-Emek.

"The Jewish Agency is assigning you to different places," he said.

"But why? We're happy here," Alitash protested.

"You've done so well—"

"Is that it?" Daniel asked. "We have to suffer because we've done well?"

Emanuel shook his head, unable to explain the mysterious ways of bureaucracy.

"Really, I don't know why they're separating you. Maybe it's because more and more young people are coming from Ethiopia, and they want to send them to this *ulpan* because it's one of the best. Maybe they think if they separate you, you'll become absorbed even faster." He shrugged his shoulders sadly.

Alitash was sent to Hazorea, three miles from Mishmar Ha-Emek, and Daniel to a village near Gedera on the coast.

For Alitash, alone for the first time without family or friends, the next six months seemed the longest and the loneliest in her life. She worked hard, improving her Hebrew, taking her turn in the kitchen, the dining hall, the nursery, the sewing room, the fields. She was learning a lot, she realized, but at what cost? The happy outgoing girl who had left Weleka was now a sad and depressed young woman. She walked through the kibbutz for hours alone, wondering how anyone in the world could smile.

Late on a Friday afternoon, Daniel appeared. Except for his dark-ivory skin, he looked like a native-born Israeli. His small mustache was now large and bristling. He wore jeans, an open-collared shirt, and sturdy brown shoes.

They embraced and kissed three times, four times, five times. Alitash tried to lose herself in his arms. Finally, Daniel looked at her. "Alitash, your eyes are red."

She sniffed quickly, determined not to let him see her cry. "What is it?" he asked.

She blurted out, "I'm so homesick, Dani. I miss my mother. And I feel so guilty. She'll never forgive me for leaving her. And I miss you. I can't tell you how much I miss you." She turned her face away from him.

Daniel held her close to his body. "I miss you too, Alitash.

I think so often of when we were together crossing mountains and rivers. We'll always be together, whatever lies ahead for us."

His fingers moved gently over her closed eyes.

"What should we do?" she asked.

"I'll try to see Emanuel. Maybe he can arrange something so we can be together again."

"I can't bear to be without you anymore."

He stroked her black hair. "I love you, Alitash. You know that. You're part of my life. The most important part."

A few weeks later, Emanuel drove to Kibbutz Hazorea and looked for Alitash. He found her in the nursery taking care of the children.

"You don't need a kibbutz anymore. We're sending you, and most of the group you came with, to Ashdod."

"Daniel too?"

"Of course."

THE ISRAEL OF the kibbutz had been a friendly, protected life in a pastoral setting. It was stage one in the odyssey of their absorption. For Alitash, coming out of a mud house in a mud village, it had been a magical entrance, not without pain, into the twentieth century.

Life in Ashdod was to be stage two. Ashdod was a city of concrete, with high-tech industries, frozen-food factories, pharmaceutical houses, movie theaters, filling stations, cafés, apartment houses, and ships sailing in and out of the busy harbor on the Mediterranean.

Emanuel drove the little group through the city to a hostel, and showed them their separate rooms. Each room had a bare cot, a small desk, and a hard chair. The girls were to live on one floor, the boys on another.

"Here in Ashdod," Emanuel explained to them as they sat in the simple dining room, "we want you to continue to study, take courses, learn new skills. Each of you will get a stipend every month from the Jewish Agency. Here you'll be much more on your own than in the kibbutzim."

The girls were enrolled in a one-year course to become day-care-center workers. Some of the boys went to vocational schools. Daniel was accepted in the preparatory year program of the Beersheba Technical College, studying electronics. Shmuel, Yael's boyfriend, and several of the others went into the army, determined to enter fighting units as soon as possible.

Within days, they were discovered by Sarah Levin.

Sarah was a small, motherly woman, with short hair, a round face, a bustling manner, and dangling earrings. At twenty-one, with a teaching degree, Sarah had come here alone in 1959 from Chicago. After a few years, she married an Israeli who was now the chief accountant for the Ashdod electronics division of the booming aeronautics industry. Their two daughters, from a comfortable middle-class home, had both chosen to live like early pioneers. Naavah was in a new kibbutz in the Galilee, Yael in the Negev, and Sarah worried about them both living in kibbutzim surrounded by Arabs.

In Ashdod, Sarah had power. She was the Ashdod executive director of Na'amat, the Pioneer Women's Organization, and an elected member of the Central Committee of the Labor Party.

In 1977, Sarah was approached by a representative of the Ministry of Immigrant Absorption. "The first groups of Ethiopian Jews are arriving," he told her. "We're organizing volunteers all over the country to work with them. We need some in Ashdod, and Sarah, you've done so much volunteering—" He stopped. "I don't know whether to call you a professional volunteer or a lay professional."

Sarah smiled wryly. "Maybe both."

"We'd like you to be one of our chief volunteers."

Sarah readily agreed.

Twelve families had arrived at once; six were widows with

little children. The rest were young parents with children, aunts and uncles, and grandparents. None spoke English. But Sarah, with sign language and good will, made herself understood and helped settle them in apartments in Ashdod.

Now, learning that a group of young people had arrived, Sarah entered the hostel, introduced herself to Alitash and Daniel and the others, and offered to help. In a few days, knowing the girls were in Israel without their mothers, Sarah "adopted" Alitash, Yael, and Malka.

She scrounged through her closets, and brought them clothes and curtains and warm blankets. Often on Saturdays, her three Ethiopian daughters came to her apartment, ate a warm lunch, then relaxed in her living room.

On Shabbat, Alitash could block out some of her loneliness and her guilt. She could even overcome her reticence and talk to Sarah about her fears for her family and her recurrent nightmares, since her letters went unanswered, that maybe her parents were dead.

At last, toward the middle of 1981, a letter reached her from home. "Dear Alitash," her twelve-year-old sister wrote, "we received your letter, and were very glad. Where is Ashdod? Mother has given birth to a little boy. He is a good baby. Thank God, we are all well. How are you?"

Alitash read and reread the letter. She could see the whole family hovering over the new baby. She could see her mother nursing him, and her father smiling with pride. Another son!

That evening she showed the letter to Daniel.

"I should be celebrating. I should be singing, 'I have a new brother.' But I can't. I miss them so much . . ." Her voice trailed off.

"At least you know your family's safe," Daniel said. "I wish all of us could find out how our families are. Things are bad in Ethiopia."

"What do you mean?"

"I heard in school today that Major Malaku has driven ORT out of Ethiopia."

"Why?" Alitash asked in dismay.

"Because ORT is a *Jewish* organization."

"But he let ORT stay even when he was arresting the teachers."

"He says ORT was involved in *aliyah*. He says ORT people helped smuggle Jewish students out. It doesn't matter to him that ORT did all those things—dug wells, hired teachers, even gave the Christian and Moslem farmers money for oxen and seed. So now the Christians and Moslems will suffer along with our people."

Alitash covered her face with her hands. "Is there anybody left in Ethiopia who can help Jews?"

Daniel shook his head. "Nobody."

IN THE NEXT months, Major Malaku ordered the synagogues closed. Entering a Jewish village, he burned two hundred Hebrew books, among them the sacred Orit, the Bible written by hand on goatskin. Like his Soviet mentors, he forbade teaching Hebrew. That Hebrew was the official language of a sovereign nation was irrelevant. Men caught teaching the outlawed language were arrested and tortured.

In Sarah's office, Alitash read the newspaper account of Malaku's newest anti-Semitic violence. She shivered as if she were in a theater of barbarism.

"Why is he doing all these terrible things now?" Alitash finally put the newspaper down on the desk. "He's already thrown ORT out. He's already tortured the teachers. Why does he need to do more atrocities?"

"It's obvious," Sarah answered. "He wants to frighten the Jews. He wants to prevent them from trying to leave Ethiopia, and come here, the way you came."

"But if he hates the Jews, why does he want to keep them there? Oh, Sarah. I'm so worried. Half my heart is here and half is in Ethiopia."

Sarah took Alitash's hands in both of hers. "It's not only

happening in Ethiopia. Look at the terrorists. They sneak into Israel. They bomb our airports and buses. They throw grenades in our schools. They kill our children. People think terrorists are only against Israel. It's not so. They're against all Jews. They'd like to see us all dead."

"We've got to do something," Alitash said in despair.

Four months later, in December 1981, hundreds of Ethiopians marched on Jerusalem.

"Rescue our brothers and sisters," Emanuel pleaded, speaking for the marchers at the rally. "Rescue them, before it's too late."

NEARLY A year passed.

Alitash sat in Sarah's living room, staring out the window.

"What's wrong, *motek* [darling]?" Sarah asked.

Alitash stroked the head of Sarah's dog. "I don't want to trouble you."

"You can tell me."

"Things are not good. Not the way I thought they would be."

"Why? I thought you were making such a good adjustment. I hear you're doing very well at the day-care-center course. You speak Hebrew as if you were born here. You keep your room at the hostel spotless. I'm proud of you."

"Sarah, I'm so lonely, sometimes I think I want to die."

There had already been two suicides among the Ethiopians. One was an emotionally disturbed young man who had been hospitalized. He found a white girlfriend who, after a bitter argument, screamed, "You can go to hell." In Ethiopia, this was not an ill-tempered outcry. It was a terrible curse. He broke down, was readmitted to the hospital, and hanged himself. Another was a youngster in the school at Mikveh Israel who had failed a test. He went down to the cellar of the school, found an electric cord, and also hanged himself.

"You don't really mean you want to die." Sarah squeezed

the hands she was holding. "Honey, I think you're feeling so bad because you miss your family."

"I dream about them nearly every night. But that's not why I feel like dying."

"What is it, then?"

"It's Daniel. He's away most of the time in that school in Beersheba."

Sarah looked at her nineteen-year-old Ethiopian daughter as if she were seeing her with fresh eyes. "Why don't you and Daniel get married? You're both so in love."

"We'd like to get married. But we have no money. Just the stipends we get from the Jewish Agency."

"Think about it, Alitash. We'll all help you."

"I will think about it. I will talk to Daniel. He must think about it too."

Daniel returned to Ashdod for the weekend. Alitash greeted him as he entered the hostel.

"Let's go for a walk," she said. "I have much to tell you."

They walked on a concrete street, as once they had walked in the tree-laced highlands of Gondar. High-rise buildings with balconies, massive white in the Mediterranean sun, towered over them as they sat on a stone bench. Across the broad thoroughfare, children romped through a modernistic playground, crawling in and out of flaming-orange concrete igloos, swinging on rubber tires.

"Daniel," Alitash began, "do you remember when Emanuel drove us that first day? He said they want us to become independent Israelis."

"I remember."

"I want that, Dani. I want to become an independent Israeli. Now."

Daniel turned on the bench to stare at her. "It will be months before you become a day-care worker."

"I'm going to quit the course. There are too many of us taking it already. They don't have enough day-care centers to give us all jobs. I think it's a way to keep us studying until they know what to do with us."

"And if you quit, what will you do?"

"I'll get a job. There are a lot of factories in Ashdod. I'll get work."

"Alitash, you never had a job in your life."

"You think I can't do it! You think because Jewish girls in Ethiopia never worked outside their houses, I can't work here."

"What's behind this, Alitash? What are you trying to tell me?"

"That I love you, Daniel"—the words spilled out—"and I want us to get married, and I'll work and support us both so you can finish your studies, and that's what I want to do, and you mustn't stop me."

Daniel put his arms around her. "Set the day."

THE WEDDING WAS in Ashdod's Canada House Absorption Center. More than two hundred guests, nearly all of them Ethiopians, were invited. Sarah arranged it with her Na'amat volunteers.

Everything fell into place. First Alitash found a job assembling small parts in a local electronics plant called Vichey Israel.

Through the Jewish Agency, Sarah found a sunny two-bedroom apartment for the young couple in one of Ashdod's best neighborhoods. The Jewish Agency gave them the loan to buy furniture.

In a friend's house, Sarah found an unused desk and bookcase. One of the first books Daniel placed in his new bookcase was an English text called *Electrical Engineering Technician*. His abilities in electrical engineering had been recognized; he was admitted to the prestigious ORT Sigalovsky School in Tel Aviv. His three-year army service was postponed to allow him to finish his training.

With the wedding day approaching, Sarah piled Alitash into her little car and drove to a bridal shop. Alitash tried on a soft white lace gown that flowed with the curves of her body. A lace ruffle high around her neck framed her face. They rented the gown and with it the bridal veil and a crown of white flowers to wear in her hair.

"Alitash." Sarah stood back admiringly. "You're going to be the most beautiful bride in Ashdod."

Alitash shook her head. "If only my family . . ."

"I know, honey. But just think how happy they'll be when you write them that you and Daniel are married."

They entered a shoe store and fitted Alitash into a pair of white satin high-heeled shoes, the first high heels she had ever worn. She stumbled across the floor to a low mirror and smiled.

The next afternoon, they helped Daniel buy his first suit, a white shirt, and a blue tie. "Dashing," Sarah approved. "Like a movie star."

Finally, befitting the mother of the bride, she bought herself a silk print dress, a matching silk jacket, and a new pair of dangling earrings.

The morning before the wedding, Alitash went to the *mikvah*, the ceremonial bath. She showered, scrubbed her whole body, shampooed her hair, cut her nails, then stepped into the *mikvah* pool for the ceremony of purification. She observed the ritual, immersing her whole body in water, excitedly, willingly, for the most important event of her life.

The wedding day dawned bright and full of promise. In the afternoon, Sarah took a group of her Na'amat volunteers to decorate the lobby of Canada House. They set up small tables with white tablecloths and red roses in the center. They piled a long table framed against the wall with Israeli salads, cold cuts, tall bottles of Coke and other soft drinks, stacks of injera bread, and a three-layered wedding cake trimmed with flowers and cherries, a cake such as no one in Ethiopia had ever seen.

The guests began arriving early in the evening. Yael, Malka, Shmuel, and all the young people who had made the trek together to Sudan were among the first to enter. Emanuel drove from Jerusalem with his wife, a former American social worker; friends came from Jerusalem and Tel Aviv, from Beersheba and Ashkelon, and from the kibbutzim where they had begun their absorption into Israel. The older women were draped in white shammas, the younger ones in Israeli dresses, the men in jeans or army uniforms. They sat on chairs against the wall, chatting in low voices, waiting for the ceremony to begin.

In the new apartment, Sarah helped Alitash into her wedding gown. "You have *kalah-chen* [the beauty of a bride]," she said.

Alitash caught her face in the small mirror on the wall. The delicate white lace ruffling around her throat, the white flowers in her black curly hair, the white veil cascading to her shoulders made her copper skin golden. Her luminous eyes sparkled.

Alitash drew herself to her full height, picked up her bridal corsage of white roses tied with white satin, and drove with Sarah to Canada House.

Dapper in his gray suit, Daniel was already in the lobby discussing the wedding procedure with two men—the rabbi, Avraham Blu Yitzhak Cohen, an Ashkenazi rabbi dressed in a black suit and a black hat, and Aryeh Azoulai, the mayor of Ashdod.

The rabbi and the mayor led Daniel to a small table and showed him the *ketubah*, the wedding certificate that Daniel would present to his bride.

"The *ketubah* is how we protect Jewish women," the rabbi explained to Daniel, who had never been to a typical Israeli wedding. "The idea of protecting women this way with a written document goes all the way back to Talmudic days."

The rabbi carefully inscribed on the certificate a nominal sum of money that Daniel would give Alitash if she were to be widowed or divorced. Whatever dowry Alitash brought, he promised in the document to return that money too.

Daniel chuckled. Alitash had no dowry, and he had nothing he could promise to give her. But he liked the idea of a marriage certificate protecting Alitash. In Ethiopia too, there would have been a marriage certificate. There he would have worn a red and white band around his forehead as a symbol of his and Alitash's purity, and his best friend would have carried Alitash on his back to present her to Daniel.

Suddenly, the people began clapping, singing, shouting joyously in Amharic and Hebrew. Alitash had entered.

Daniel walked toward her, his eyes riveted. "You're beautiful. Even more beautiful than the day we bought you your shamma in Gondar."

Gondar! How far she had come since that day in the Gondar market. A thousand miles in space; a thousand years in time. Transported from the middle ages to the twentieth century. Catapulted from the mud village of Weleka to Ashdod.

Daniel led her toward the *chuppah*—the bridal canopy. Four of their friends held it aloft on wooden poles.

Under the *chuppah*, with Sarah, as her surrogate mother, holding one arm and Yael the other, Alitash walked seven times around Daniel. His eyes glistened with love.

Rabbi Cohen then recited the blessings of the betrothal. "May He Who is supreme power, blessing, and glory bless this bridegroom and bride."

The rabbi sanctified a goblet of wine, and handed it first to Daniel who sipped it, and then, lifting Alitash's veil, pressed it to her lips.

Daniel then placed the gold wedding band on Alitash's finger, repeating the words after the rabbi: "By this ring you are consecrated to me as my wife in accordance with the law of Moses and Israel."

Alitash looked at Daniel through her veil and knew that she would love him to the end of days.

Rabbi Cohen read the words on the *ketubah*. "Be thou my wife according to the law of Moses. I faithfully promise that I will be a true husband unto thee and I will honor and cherish thee."

Mayor Azoulai was given the honor of sharing in the reading of the "Seven Blessings." Alitash and Daniel felt the words might have been written for them: "May Zion rejoice as her children are restored to her in joy. Praised are You, O Lord, who causes Zion to rejoice at her children's return."

We are the children, Alitash thought, *the children who have returned*.

Once again the rabbi handed Daniel the glass goblet of wine Daniel sipped it, then carefully he lifted Alitash's veil and gave it to her to drink.

Now the rabbi placed the empty glass under Daniel's foot to stomp on and shatter. Even on this night, he was not to forget the destruction of the Temple in Jerusalem in the year A.D. 70. And Daniel trod on the glass, promising to remember..

The shouts rang across the hall. *"Mazal Tov. Mazal Tov."*

Alitash and Daniel kissed. The guests in shammas and jeans crowded around them, hugging and kissing them both in Israeli and Ethiopian style. At the tables with the red roses, they dined on the Ethiopian injera, the Israeli cold cuts and salads, and the three-tiered wedding cake. Alitash and Daniel sat at the head table smiling like royalty.

Sarah had arranged cassettes of music with a tape recorder. She switched on the tapes. Soon the whole audience was on the floor, holding hands in a circle, shammas flying, dancing the hora.

Then came the Ethiopian music, with its strong rhythmic beat. Two men in jeans and cotton shirts stood up, clapping their hands first slowly, tentatively, with the audience clapping with them. Then the two men placed their hands on their thighs, shaking their shoulders, gyrating, preening like birds in a forest, shaking wilder and wilder. More men joined them, dancing until they were ready to drop with exhaustion. Soon little children were on the floor, shaking their shoulders, gyrating, preening, laughing, while their parents and the whole assembly looked on with delight.

Long past midnight, Sarah drove the bridal couple to their new apartment.

Daniel led Alitash into the bedroom. "Come sit here on the side of the bed with me," he said.

He opened the Bible to the songs that were Solomon's. Alitash, suffused with love, listened as he read to her.

> *"My beloved spake, and said unto me:*
> *'Rise up, my love, my fair one,*
> *and come away. . . .*
> *Arise, my love, my fair one. . . .' "*

He put his arms gently around her and drew her to him.

Chapter Twelve

IN SUDAN IN April 1985, President Gaafar el-Nimeiri's sixteen-year rule came to an abrupt and ignominious end.

Nimeiri was off on a mission to Washington asking for more aid. His absence from Sudan may have helped his downfall; it undoubtedly saved his life.

Arrested and imprisoned, Major General Omar Mohammed el-Tayeb, the former first vice president, and four aides were charged with treason and spying, instigating war against the state, and undermining the constitution.

Their four-month trial became the hottest game in town. Pictures of the trial were broadcast every night on Khartoum television. Each day Israel and the United States were denounced on the streets and in the press for daring to rescue Ethiopian Jews.

The prosecution alleged that the airlift had been masterminded by the U.S. embassy in Sudan and that the CIA had paid Tayeb $2 million "as an installment for his services." The money, the prosecutor charged, came from "Jewish organizations concerned with Jewish resettlement."

U.S. officials lodged an official complaint, denouncing the charges as a distortion of the humanitarian goal of the airlift.

A million dollars had indeed been spent in Sudan to rescue the Jews; but the U.S. pointed out that the money had gone, not into General el-Tayeb's pocket, but to pay for the trucks and buses, the gasoline and food and safe houses, and the security needed to airlift over seven thousand people.

In January 1986, el-Tayeb was found guilty and given a thirty year prison term and a life sentence, to be served consecutively. Pressure from the West did much to prevent him from being hanged. On April 11, 1987, a Sudanese court reduced his sentence to ten years.

MEANWHILE ACROSS the border in Ethiopia, in the wake of the sensational trial in Sudan and the end of Operation Moses, the plight of the Jews deteriorated.

Most of the eight-to-ten thousand were elderly or mothers with infants and young children. The rest were the sick, the crippled, the disabled who had been unable to make the trek to Sudan.

Missing were the young men who once had helped their fathers plant the seed and harvest the crops. They were now in Israel.

The village girls, coming of marriageable age, began to fear a future without husbands.

Sickness stalked the villages—dysentery, malaria, tuberculosis, malnutrition. Children whose bones were so soft they could not stand up and walk, crawled on sticklike hands and twisted feet. With only rags to cover them, many shivered in the rainstorms, trying to keep warm by embracing themselves as they raced barefoot searching for food.

With no running water, no sanitation, and flies roosting on the eyes of adults as well as children, whole villages developed conjunctivitis. Conjunctivitis led to trachoma. Trachoma led to glaucoma. Glaucoma led to blindness.

"In Ethiopia," Rabbi Yosef Hadani, the first Ethiopian ordained outside of Ethiopia, told me, "most of the people are elderly and their children cannot help them anymore, because their children are in Israel. The Jewish schools are all closed. The children who study in government schools get only a Communist education—and I don't know what will happen to them if we don't save them soon."

Major Malaku had now been promoted and was head of the Communist Party for the whole province. He ordered guards and roadblocks to cordon off the Jewish villages, lest tourists bring some help to the people. In 1985, no foreigners were allowed to enter a single Jewish village.

A bureaucratic tug-of-war flared up between Malaku and the National Tour Operation (NTO), desperate to revive the once flourishing tourist trade. For years, Jewish travelers from America and Europe had come to Ethiopia and flown on little planes from Addis up to Gondar. They had entered the Jewish villages, brought books and Torahs and religious articles for the people, bought pottery and handicrafts, and left hard currency behind.

Now, with tourists barred, the luxury Gohar Hotel in Gondar would have gone bankrupt if it were not owned by the government.

In the summer of 1986, the NTO won the tug-of-war. A small group of American Jewish visitors, brought together by the North American Conference on Ethiopian Jewry (NACOEJ), was given permission to enter five Jewish villages. Led by NACOEJ's chairman, Barbara Ribakove, they were accompanied everywhere by government tourist guides and security personnel.

Knowing the needs of the villagers, the Americans brought

cartons of medicines, clothing, and hundreds of ball-point pens, too costly for most Ethiopian schoolchildren. Elsie Roth, a public health nurse from St. Louis, organized the travelers into instant health-care workers and taught them how to squeeze antibiotic salves into the people's eyes.

Delighted with their visitors, the people rushed back inside their tukuls and brought out photos their children had sent them from Israel.

Some smiled proudly as they showed the pictures. Others wept. In each village, the unspoken questions hung in the air—would they ever see their children again? Would their families ever be whole again?

"Don't forget us," they pleaded.

In Amharic, in Hebrew, in sign language, they asked their new friends to snap pictures of them holding the photos of their children against their chests.

The visitors took Polaroid pictures, gave some to the parents, and brought the rest to the children in Israel.

In Ashdod, Alitash, heavy with child, kissed and then wept over the pictures of her mother looking forlorn, of her father and sister and the little brother she had never seen. Had her mother forgiven her? Would she ever see her family again?

SITTING AT HER office window, Sarah Levin watched the late afternoon sun suffusing Ashdod's skyline.

She leaned back in her chair, thinking of her three Ethiopian daughters, Alitash, Yael, and Malka. She had helped arrange their weddings, and each one was now holding a job.

This is absorption, she thought. They have become full-fledged Israelis. Alitash was a skilled worker in the Vichey Israel electronics factory. Yael was a translator in the hospital in Ashkelon. Malka was a translator-counselor in the Ashkelon Absorption Center.

Their husbands too were making it in Israel. Daniel was excelling in the ORT school in Tel Aviv. Shmuel, Yael's husband, and Shlomo, who had come several years earlier and fallen in love with the beautiful Malka at first sight, were both finishing their army stints.

Sarah shut her eyes.

What was it back there in Ethiopia that made these young people such *Menschen*—decent, responsible, caring human beings? What was it their parents had taught them? Was it their culture, their closeness, their love of family, their need for each other to survive? If only they can keep those qualities here—

Her thoughts were interrupted by a knock on the door. "May I come in?" It was Alitash.

Sarah jumped from her chair to kiss her. "How do you feel?"

"Fine. Well, maybe a little tired. It was a busy day at the factory. I was just in the mood to see you."

"Let's go down and have coffee."

In a small sidewalk café, they sipped hot coffee.

"Eat something, Alitash," Sarah said. "You're eating now for two."

Alitash let Sarah order a cheese Danish. She took a few bites, then put it down. "I'm full of guilt, Sarah."

"Did something happen between you and Daniel?"

"No, no. Not with Daniel. I can't believe sometimes how much in love we are. No, Sarah, it's guilt about my family. Now that I'm going to have my own baby, the guilt is worse."

She opened her purse and drew out the Polaroid picture of her mother.

"Your mother is beautiful," Sarah said.

Tears formed behind Alitash's eyes. "I see the pictures on television of the people starving in Ethiopia. I want to turn off the TV, and then I can't . . ."

Sarah reached across the table to touch Alitash's hand. "You're torturing yourself."

"I put aside money from my salary. Every month now I go to the bank and send fifty American dollars to my parents. They write me. They get the money. But I don't know if it's enough to feed them. Everything is so expensive there now. Oxen and seed cost four and five times more than they used to. The famine is moving toward them. I hear seven million people were affected by the famine so far, and a million died. Sarah, if they die, I will never forgive myself for leaving them."

"Listen to me, my darling. You're suffering from something the psychologists call 'survivor guilt.' It's what many who survived the Holocaust in Europe go through. They torment themselves—why am I alive and not my father? Why I and not my mother, my husband, my wife, my children? Why didn't they burn me in a gas chamber? Why did I survive?"

Alitash listened. "That's exactly what I ask myself. Why am I alive? Why am I here? Why do I have enough to eat? Sometimes the pain stabs me like a knife in my stomach. I'm afraid it will affect my baby inside."

"Maybe it's time you stopped working."

"No. I'm going to work right up to the day I deliver. I have to."

"Alitash, you amaze me more every day. You work hard at the factory, then you go home, market, cook, do the laundry, and keep your house cleaner even than you kept your little room in the hostel."

Alitash looked at her watch. "I better get home right away. I have to start cooking dinner, and I haven't done the laundry yet. Come with me for a while. Dani's studying for his exams. He'd love to see you."

They drove to Alitash's apartment, now fully furnished with an upholstered sofa, a matching love seat, an armchair, and a coffee table. Draperies framed the windows, and filling a corner of the living room was the television set, with a radio and tape recorder and cassettes with Ethiopian music.

Alitash hurried into the bedroom to change her clothes. Sarah walked into the kitchen and stopped abruptly. Food was bubbling on the stove. On a small table, laundry was neatly stacked.

Daniel came into the kitchen to greet her.

218

"What's going on here?" Sarah asked.

"Nothing," Daniel said. "I finished the laundry and I started the cooking."

Sarah put her hands on her hips. "Did your father do this in Ethiopia?"

He stroked his mustache.

"Did my mother work in an electronics factory?"

A FEW MONTHS later, Sarah was in her living room pasting an album with pictures of her three black granddaughters. Alitash's little girl Orly, whose name meant "My Light," had a round copper-gold face. Her body was chubby, her thighs so fat Sarah could hardly get her hands around them.

Yael's little daughter was named Shulamit for the black and comely Shulamit of the Song of Songs.

Malka's little girl Ricky, the oldest of the three, was a born tomboy.

Sarah tried to analyze for herself the secret of their good absorption into Israel. They had been here nearly five years. They had come in a small group. Not en masse, like the thousands who had come on Operation Moses.

Maybe, she thought, maybe because my three girls did come in a small group, they could be absorbed more readily. Maybe it was because in Ashdod we put two or three Ethiopian families in apartment houses with twenty or thirty other families. As a small group, they were not seen as a threat by anyone. And, with Ethiopian friends living in similar houses nearby, they had their own support system.

Maybe also, she thought, it's because their children are so easily integrated into the schools. Whenever she had time, she dropped in at the day-care centers run by her Na'amat organization, delighting in the sight of her Ethiopian grandchildren flying down a sliding pond, drinking juice, spreading blankets on the floor and napping side by side with children from India, Iran, America, Russia, Israel.

On one of her free days, she took the three children of one of Alitash's friends to the zoo near Tel Aviv. They were ten, seven, and four years old, and she knew they were lively and irrepressible.

Sarah warned them, "Promise you'll sit quietly in the car. Otherwise I can't drive, and we can't go." They promised.

In the zoo, several people stopped to stare at them. A woman holding two blond, blue-eyed girls by the hand walked up to Sarah. "Are these children new immigrants?" she asked.

"New immigrants!" Sarah repeated. "They were born in Israeli beds, like your children and mine. They go to Israeli schools. They speak Hebrew. It's the only language they know, and this is the only world they know. It's their land too."

"I'm sorry. I didn't mean to insult you." The woman hurried away.

Sarah was annoyed. But not the children. They were sabra children with sabra *chuzpa*.

"I don't like the zebra." Ruhama, the seven-year-old, looked disdainfully at the striped animals. "I don't like zebras altogether."

"Why?"

"They can't make up their minds if they're black or white."

"Ruhama, does anybody every say anything to you in school about your color?" Sarah asked.

"Only once. A boy in my class called me *cushi* [black]."

"And what did you do?"

Ruhama tossed her head. "Cheese is white. So I called him 'cheese.' Nobody ever called me *cushi* again."

Chapter Thirteen

Y ONA BEN NAFTALI'S absorption was different.

On his arrival, he had been greeted with the honors befitting an elder statesman, especially a statesman rescued from
imminent arrest.

Then, like all newcomers, he was given immediate citizen-
ship and the rights of a new immigrant. He needed no absorption center and no volunteers to help him begin his new life.
He spoke Hebrew fluently.

His long years of work, incurring the wrath of Haile Selassie
so he could serve Jewish children, were recognized by the
government and the Jewish Agency. He was given a three-
room apartment in a modest neighborhood in Petah Tikva,
and a small pension.

Within days, his fare paid by the American Association for Ethiopian Jews, he was sent to Canada to be the featured speaker at the General Assembly of the Council of Jewish Federations. He was applauded and lionized.

Then he was all but forgotten.

His destiny was not unlike that of many Zionist leaders who had come to Israel after the state was born.

In their own lands in Europe and America, they had been men and women of fame and prestige; they had fought political battles, organizing rallies, making speeches, raising funds, debating Arabs and anti-Zionists. Then they came to Israel, expecting to participate in the country's political life. Instead, they found themselves unwanted and unneeded in the corridors of power. Israeli politics had no room for them, and Israeli citizens had little time.

The English dealt with the problem of superannuated leaders by creating a House of Lords.

Israel had only its one house, the Knesset. What it needed was a House of Heroes.

Lonely and disappointed, many lived out their lives in old-age homes. Yona at least had his own apartment with his wife Tourou and their daughter Judith. Each day Yona's six sons came to visit. Four worked in absorption centers, and two worked in banks.

Still, fear for the lives of the guarantors in Ethiopia hung over the family.

Yona's guarantor had disappeared. But no one knew the fate of the two guarantors for Tourou and Judith. The visas were good for only three months., It was now five months since they had come.

"Judith and I are going back to Addis," Tourou announced one day. "If we don't, our guarantors . . ."

Yona struggled for breath. "But how will you live?"

"We still have our house in Addis."

"How will you eat? You have no money."

"Judith will go back to her job."

"What if you get an attack? You can't be alone while she's at work. If you're determined to go, I'm going with you."

"Yona, have you lost your senses? They would arrest you the moment you landed."

"I can't bear to think of what they can do to you and Judith." The words came slowly.

"I'll tell them I was sick."

"You're still sick. Your diabetes is worse than ever."

"They'll be able to see I'm telling the truth."

"And after you're there, what then?"

Tourou shook her head. "I'm torn, Yona. How can I leave you—a sick man? Yet how can I live with myself if they kill my guarantor? Judith and I have to go back, Yona. We can't let them kill our guarantors."

Tourou and Judith returned to Ethiopia. At the airport in Addis, the immigration authorities accepted Tourou's explanation that sickness had kept her from returning, and that her daughter Judith had stayed to take care of her.

Their guarantors were safe.

WITH TOUROU gone, two of Yona's unmarried sons came to live with him—Yehuda, his youngest, and Jeremiah.

Jeremiah, who had survived the May Day massacre, had gone into the army, finished his stint, and was now working as a cashier in a bank. Each afternoon he hung up his banking clothes, stepped into black silk shorts, an open-collared shirt, and sandals, and did the family cooking.

"Jeremiah is my master chef," Yona boasted as they served the food to friends who came with newspapers and flowers and love. Young women, studying at the Hebrew University in Jerusalem, traveled by bus on Friday afternoons to spend Shabbat with Yona and his sons.

Yona's health began to improve a little. He was asked to contribute articles to a small periodical called the *Voice of Israel* published by the Knesset-sponsored National Council for Ethiopian Jews and handwritten in Amharic. The paper was to help explain life in Israel to newcomers who had not yet learned to read Hebrew.

Yona found gratification in being a teacher again, teaching through his articles.

Meanwhile Tourou made the rounds of the government in Ethiopia asking for a permanent exit visa to take care of her husband. But the visa did not come.

Yona's asthma grew worse. Every few months, he was rushed to the hospital unable to breathe.

Jeremiah wrote to his mother in Addis.

"Father is in the hospital again, so weak he can't hold food. He talks so low we can barely understand him. We are afraid he is close to death. Try to come as soon as possible. Don't wait for a permanent exit. Take whatever time they will give you. But come."

Unlike the "wedding" invitation, this letter was true.

Jeremiah's letter succeeded.

Tourou again found someone willing at great personal risk to be her guarantor. With an exit visa for three months, she flew to Kenya and on to Israel, rushing to Yona's side.

Under her ministrations, Yona grew stronger, yet not strong enough for her to leave him in three months.

A year passed. Then two years. Both were not well.

Tourou controlled her diabetes with daily insulin shots, but she was tormented.

"Yona," she said at last, "I can't stay any longer. I must go back. I can't risk my guarantor's life."

Yona struggled for breath. "But without you . . ." He could not go on.

"I know, Yona," Tourou said. "You need me, and I need you. But what if they kill my guarantor?"

Yona was silent for a while. Then he said, "Talk to the authorities in Ethiopia. Talk about the reunification of families. Maybe this time they'll give you a visa to join me for good."

Arriving at the airport in Addis, Tourou was confronted by an angry immigration official.

"For not returning when you should have, you are fined fifteen thousand birr [$7,500]."

"Fifteen thousand birr." Tourou was aghast. "You might as well ask for a million."

He shrugged his shoulders. "Pay it or else."

"Or else," Tourou knew, meant they could imprison her. But at least her guarantor was safe.

Yona appealed to his friends in Israel and America to help raise the funds to keep Tourou out of jail.

The American Association for Ethiopian Jews provided the money. Tourou paid the fine and then applied for a permanent exit visa.

A year passed. Then two years. It was now 1987.

Each day Yona took to his bed praying that Tourou would get permission to join him in Israel before it was too late for them both, praying too that the thousands of Jews still in Ethiopia would be rescued and absorbed.

Yona knew the daring and courage it had taken to bring in the fifteen thousand who were now in Israel. But he knew also, from his own experience, that absorbing people was far more complicated than rescuing them.

He knew there was a kind of timetable for absorption.

Absorption was easiest for children up to the age of eighteen.

From eighteen to twenty-five, it was more difficult, but could still be successful.

From twenty-five to thirty-five, it was far more difficult.

From thirty-five on, it was often hopeless. Many would probably be dependent on the state for the rest of their lives.

This, he knew, was the pattern of all immigration. In Israel, as in America, grandparents rarely learned to speak the language. And if they found work, it was usually menial.

Yona foresaw a long-drawn-out process of successes and failures, of trial and error.

A prime example was the experiment at the Princess Hotel

in the lively resort town of Netanya. It was one of nine hotels the Jewish Agency had leased in the hectic days of Operation Moses. Eighty families, 370 people in all, lived in the Princess Hotel's bedrooms.

With no place to cook and no place to congregate, women often spent hours lying across the beds. Children of school age attended the public schools of Netanya, but when they came back, they turned the hotel's narrow corridors into playgrounds. Little girls sat, sad-eyed, against the corridor walls, tending their mothers' babies.

The Princess Hotel was a disaster and its Israeli-born director, Leah von Weisel, whom everyone called "Lucy," was the first to admit it. She was a short, softly rounded woman with a cigarette almost permanently fixed in her right hand.

From the start, Lucy realized that a hotel was no place for families, especially families who had come out of villages where they had their own homes, however small and humble.

It was not that the Jewish Agency didn't try. The agency genuinely wanted to give the people tools for survival. Each morning in the *ulpan*, fourteen teachers met in fourteen classes to teach the people Hebrew. Each afternoon men assembled in a workshop learning to use screwdrivers, hammers, and saws. In a fully equipped kitchen, women were taught the mysteries of a refrigerator and a stove, and how to cook Israeli-style. Mothers were taught how to take care of their infants and their small children. In a workshop, women were taught how to sew on electric sewing machines. Parasocial workers taught them how to cope with health problems, how to go to the clinic, how to find their way around Netanya.

Once a week, Lucy met with the adults to answer their questions, and to give them an introduction to Israel.

And once a week, she met with her social workers, who brought her the problems they faced. Lucy was known for her frankness. Like another chain-smoker, Golda Meir, she was determined to face tough problems and find solutions.

On a warm August morning in 1985, Lucy held a meeting

with newcomers on her staff. "Staying in this hotel is the worst thing that can happen to these people," she said.

"Worse than the camps in Sudan?" one of the young assistants asked.

"No, Sudan must have been worse. But the Princess Hotel is worse than any place in Ethiopia. I'll tell you why."

She ticked off her fingers. "First, living in a hotel turns people into a herd. In other absorption centers, they live together in families, or they're single people living with other single people. Here we have a mass of people who act, because of the situation, like a bloc. I hate it. I hate having to deal with people in a mass."

She stopped to light a new cigarette. "Second, they have lost all sense of privacy. A good part of their lives is conducted in the corridors. There's no privacy in hotel corridors. They probably had more privacy in the tukuls in Ethiopia."

"What about putting the people into tents the way they did in the 1950s?" a social worker asked. "At least until decent housing is found."

"Do you know what the world would do to us if we put people back into tents in 1985?"

She drew a deep draft of smoke through her nostrils.

"Third, they've lost their sense of responsibility for their children. They can't teach them to read and write; we're ready to do that. But they have stopped teaching them how to behave, how to obey rules."

She lit a new cigarette on the butt of the old one.

"I'll go on. Fourth, their culture in Ethiopia is circled around the family. Here they lose their family frame and culture. There are no family ties. The family is broken up. The adults lose their function. In Ethiopia, the father is the breadwinner, the mother is the family organizer. In our hotel, we see the families fall apart. Children lose their respect when they see their parents no longer functioning. In Ethiopia, the mother cooks. She has status when she cooks and feeds her family. Here she can't cook; the food is given out in the dining room.

She can't even give her husband his morning coffee—something that was very important to her in Ethiopia."

The footsteps of children racing up and down the corridor filtered through the door.

"We made a lot of mistakes. We didn't know their customs and they didn't know ours. At the beginning, we set the food before the children first, so their parents could feed them. But in Ethiopia, parents eat first. So here the parents probably thought, all right, these people want us to eat this food and then they'll bring more food for the children.

"But we were shocked. How could parents eat the food and not first feed their children? In our eyes, it seemed the parents didn't care for their children. Nobody explained the different customs to them or to us. It hurt them very much, and it hurt us too. What happens is the parents lose not only their status; they lose their respect for each other and their need for each other."

A few older members of Lucy's staff had entered the room. They nodded as she talked. She was describing their own experiences.

"The fact that they're living so close together brings jealousy, especially of the men toward their wives. A woman is not supposed to be alone with a man. But if she enters the elevator to go up to her floor and a man is in it, what is she supposed to do? Run out of the elevator? Her husband becomes jealous. The jealousy is unfounded; she's not being unfaithful. In Ethiopia, a wife can't go under a roof with another man. She can't be in a room with another man unless somebody else is there. An elevator is a room."

Lucy crushed her cigarette in the ashtray on her desk, then lit another.

"It's not acceptable among them to give orders to children who are not theirs. They can't rebuke the children who run around the corridors. The parents can't handle even their own children. After a while, the parents feel the children are the responsibility of the government, so they free themselves of all responsibility and let the children run wild. The children learn fast. They start throwing stones at other children on the street. What should we do? We have no place for children to play.

"People must have something more than we can give them here. They must have culture, something you can't get in a hotel. When you come from a society where there are no theaters, the culture lies in the habits, in the customs of the family, in the ritual of food."

Lucy paused. "People can't live only by food and bed. We have to find a solution."

"What's the solution, Lucy?" someone asked.

"There are many solutions to many problems. But the first thing I want is to close down the Princess Hotel. Close down all the hotels. They're no place to absorb people."

Within the year, the Princess Hotel was shut down. The other hotels were cleared out, one by one. The people were placed in absorption centers around the country. Families were once more kept intact.

"We don't want to make the same mistakes we made in the 1950s," said Chaim Aharon, the chairman of the Immigration and Absorption Department of the Jewish Agency.

His critics countered, "They're making exactly the same mistakes. The only difference is that this time they know it."

In the 1950s, the hope had been to absorb the great waves of immigrants in a pressure cooker. The newcomers were to emerge as instant Israelis. It didn't work. Absorption still had its own timetable.

Now the Jewish Agency sought new ways. They called in social workers, psychologists, and social anthropologists to help. For the Ethiopians had not only the problems of all immigrants; they had a special handicap. The Rabbinical Council insisted they must be reconfirmed as Jews so there would never again be a question of their Jewishness.

The men were required to undergo a ritual recircumcision, extracting a "drop of blood" from the penis.

Many of the men were furious. "If they think," several said, "that putting a needle in us makes us Jews, after all we went through to remain Jews in Ethiopia, they just don't understand us."

Most of the country agreed with the Ethiopians. The rabbis decided that the ritual circumcision was unnecessary, but they refused to give ground on the *mikvah*, the ceremony of purification.

The *mikvah* was no problem in itself. Ethiopian men were accustomed to ritual bathing in the rivers. What they resented was that after the immersion, they would be given the certificates that converts received. The rabbis argued they were doing this in the best interests of the Ethiopians—for the sake of their children, whose Judaism could then never again be questioned.

Defying the rabbis, activist Ethiopians organized a mass sit-in. For weeks, crowds of Ethiopian men, women, and children camped in front of the luxury Plaza Hotel in Jerusalem, opposite the Chief Rabbinate. They won the sympathy of Israeli journalists and artists. Something Israel had long feared seemed in the making—the *Kulturkampf*—the battle between the small minority of Israelis who were ultra-Orthodox and the majority who were secular and nonobservant.

The sit-in was finally called off, with the issue of the ritual immersion still unresolved.

EACH MORNING IN the Beersheba Absorption Center, Ezekiel carried his crippled grandfather down the steps to attend the *ulpan* class.

Ezekiel had no problem learning Hebrew, but his grandfather struggled helplessly. He had never sat in a classroom. He had been illiterate in Ethiopia. He learned to say a few words in Hebrew, and then told Ezekiel, "It's no use. I'm too old."

"Grandfather," Ezekiel said. "You don't have to go to the

ulpan. But I must go. It's only in the morning. Then we can be together the rest of the day."

As soon as the classes ended, Ezekiel raced up the stairs to their apartment. Invariably, he found his grandfather sitting at the window watching Ethiopian children playing in the compound.

One day Ezekiel opened the door and screamed. His grandfather lay on the floor, dead.

Weeping, he lowered himself to the floor and put his head on his grandfather's chest. "I'm all alone now, Grandfather," he whispered.

"Everyone's dead. Father, Mother, now you. What will I do? Where will I go? What will happen to me?"

Then he lifted his head. The familiar sound of the children playing outside came into the room.

Through his tears he said, "You lived to see it. You and I, Grandfather. We lived to see the Holy Land."

Neighbors came to sit with Ezekiel for the *shivah*, the seven days of mourning. They tried to console him, but grief enveloped his body like a huge shamma.

When the *shivah* ended, Malka, the director of the absorption center, called him to her office.

"Ezekiel, you're too young to live here alone. We think it best for you to go to a Youth Aliyah village with other young people your age. How do you feel about it?"

Ezekiel nodded mutely.

"We're going to send you to Yemin Orde."

Yemin Orde lay high in the mountains just below Haifa. It had been named for the British General Orde Wingate who in the thirties had trained Israeli soldiers to fight Arab terrorists, and in the forties had helped drive Mussolini's army out of Ethiopia.

Midafternoon on a wintry day, Ezekiel stepped off the bus in Yemin Orde. Around him spread a seventy-acre village set in the heart of a nature preserve, with tall, protective trees, green-carpeted hills, and white cottages.

A young man met the bus and took Ezekiel to the office of Dr. Chaim Peri, the director.

"Sit down, Ezekiel," Chaim said. "I see from this paper you're alone in our country."

"Yes." Ezekiel's voice was strangled.

"You won't be alone anymore, Ezekiel. We have four hundred boys and girls here. More than a hundred are from Ethiopia. You'll meet them soon."

Ezekiel heard the words but kept his head lowered. The grief and loneliness were still in him.

Chaim continued. "You'll meet others too. Children who escaped from Syria. Children who escaped from villages in Afghanistan, villages that were wiped out by Russian planes. Some of them came with bullets in their legs. You'll meet South Americans, Europeans, even *Indians*." He smiled. "Yes, Indians. But not red Indians from America. Jewish Indians from India and Jewish Indians from Mexico. And you'll meet some children who were born right here in Israel."

Still Ezekiel said nothing, his eyes fixed blindly on the floor. Chaim stepped away from his desk. "Ezekiel, let's go look at your room."

Ezekiel followed the tall, bespectacled teacher to a dormitory cottage. The room was simple, with two single beds, two small desks, and two chairs. "This will be your room with another boy. Put your bag down, and let's walk around the village."

Chaim put his arm around Ezekiel's shoulder as they walked through the tree-lined grounds. They stopped in front of a one-room white building. "This is where you'll go to school," Chaim said. "The classes are already finished today, but if we go inside, we'll probably see some Ethiopian children still studying. They stay on after class. They're always asking their teachers for more work."

At the door, Ezekiel saw two Ethiopian boys bent over their desks, writing in notebooks. A red-haired young woman in army uniform sat between them.

232

"The teacher is a new immigrant herself," Chaim said. "Her name is Sharon and she's from Canada. She's doing her two year army service by teaching here."

Sharon looked up as they entered. "Dr. Peri," she said, "I love being here. I never met children so motivated. These boys are here a short time, and they're already speaking Hebrew as if they were born to it."

She held up one of the notebooks. "Look at this. They're writing creative stories in English."

"I know." Chaim nodded. "I've been an educator for a long time and I haven't seen anything like this in twenty years. These Ethiopian youngsters are not only bright. They've brought values here that we've long forgotten. Values like— you don't cheat, you don't lie, you don't just talk about things, you *do* them. They're going to make us very proud. Mark my words, Sharon. I think we have a future chief of staff here, maybe even a Nobel Prize winner."

Ezekiel saw the two boys smile at him, but he could not return their smile.

Chaim said, "Ezekiel, let's go on."

They entered a workshop in a white wooden building. Ezekiel saw a group of thirteen-year-old Ethiopian girls and boys. Each one sat totally absorbed in front of a keyboard and a little screen on which words and pictures were moving. They were studying math with computers programmed in English.

Outside, standing under a tree, Chaim said, "I want you to see all this, Ezekiel, not to scare you, but to show you what children are doing here and what you too can do. Over there is the soccer field. If you want to, you can be a soccer player. You can be a runner; we have a track to train runners. You can be a carpenter or an electrician, an architect or a scientist; you can learn music or act in plays or paint or photograph or be a writer. Anything, Ezekiel. You can be anything you want."

Chaim opened his hands and pressed them against Ezekiel's hands until electricity and warmth flowed between them.

Their eyes met.

"Look at us rubbing hands," Chaim said, "a man born in Israel and a boy born in Ethiopia. I am yours and you are mine. This is the meaning of Israel, Ezekiel. That we belong. We belong to each other. Here we are, from countries around the world. And we belong to each other."

He hugged Ezekiel.

Tears of joy streaked down Ezekiel's cheeks. "I have come home," he said.

The course of Ruth Gruber's career as a journalist began at age twenty-three, when the Soviets allowed her to become the first foreign correspondent to enter the Soviet Arctic. After that assignment, pioneer lands became her "beat" and were to include Alaska, Israel, Egypt, Jordan, Lebanon, Syria, Iraq, Aden, Morocco, Algeria, Tunis, Libya, Kenya, Ethiopia, Korea, Vietnam, and Puerto Rico. Her work as a foreign correspondent later led to assignments by the U.S. government, including one in 1944 by President Roosevelt that was to send her on a secret mission into Hitler's Europe—she tells the riveting tale of that journey in Haven. *Ms. Gruber has written twelve other books and lives in New York City.*